Blueprints For Advent And Christmas

Dynamic Sketches, Scenes, And Scripts For The Season

Arley K. Fadness

CSS Publishing Company, Inc., Lima, Ohio

BLUEPRINTS FOR ADVENT AND CHRISTMAS

For the history and members of Bethesda Lutheran Church in Bristol, South Dakota, who nurtured me in the faith and provided a spiritual basis for my life and ministry.

Copyright © 2008 by
CSS Publishing Company, Inc.
Lima, Ohio

The original purchaser may photocopy material in this publication for use as it was intended (worship material for worship use; educational material for classroom use; dramatic material for staging or production). No additional permission is required from the publisher for such copying by the original purchaser only. Inquiries should be addressed to: Permissions, CSS Publishing Company, Inc., 517 South Main Street, Lima, Ohio 45804.

Scripture quotations are from the New Revised Standard Version of the Bible, copyright 1989 by the Division of Christian Education of the National Council of the Churches of Christ in the USA. Used by permission.

For more information about CSS Publishing Company resources, visit our website at www.csspub.com or email us at custserv@csspub.com or call (800) 241-4056.

Cover design by Barbara Spencer
ISBN-13: 978-0-7880-2556-3
ISBN-10: 0-7880-2556-2

PRINTED IN USA

Table Of Contents

Introduction	5

Advent Midweek Worship

Advent Midweek Worship Format With Liturgical Musical Suggestions	9

Advent 1
When Israel Sang The Blues
Sketch: When Israel Sang The Blues	11
Homily: When Israel Sang The Blues	14

Advent 2
When Maiden Mary Sang The Magnificat
Sketch: When Maiden Mary Sang The Magnificat	16
Homily: When Maiden Mary Sang The Magnificat	18

Advent 3
When Teddy Roosevelt Sang Bass
Sketch: Joy To The World	20
Homily: When Teddy Roosevelt Sang Bass	22

Advent 4
When The Angels And All Creation Sang Gloria In Excelsis
Sketch: Invent and write your own
Homily: Write your own

Mini-Dramas For Cycles A And B
Cycle A

Synopses Of The Mini-Dramas For Cycle A	27
General Advent Sketch	29

Whose Birthday Is It Anyway?

Advent 1	33

Philippe

Advent 2	38

Gummy Old Men

Advent 3	42

The Water Witcher

Advent 4	47

No Clues?

Christmas Eve/Christmas Day	50

Looking For The Child Of Bethlehem

Christmas 1	55

Where's Dad?

Christmas 2	59

The Difference Between Getting And Giving

Bonus Advent Sketch	63

Prepare: An Advent Play

Cycle B

Synopses Of The Mini-Dramas For Cycle B	67
Advent 1	69
The Ball Game	
Advent 2	73
The Waiting Man	
Advent 3	77
The Waiting Room	
Advent 4	81
For What Do We Wait?	
Christmas Eve/Christmas Day	85
Stable Talk	
Christmas 1	89
Two Futures	
Christmas 2	92
The Adoption	

Additional Worship Sketches

Synopses Of Additional Worship Sketches	99
Better To Be A "Lert"	101
The Will	105
The Rabbi's Gift	109
Watching For A "Coming"	113

Outdoor Nativity Backdrop Set

Blueprint 1 — Stable Scene	119
Construction And Setup Notes For Drawings A Through N	121
Drawings A Through N	123
Photos	151

A Christmas Program

Christmas Program Format	155
Christmas Puppet Play	157
Christmas Monologues	161
Herod's Monologue	161
Innkeeper's Monologue	162
Joseph's Monologue	163
Shepherd's Monologue	164
Angel's Monologue	165
Mary's Monologue	166
Blueprint 2 — Lights And Equipment For Puppet Theatre	167

Introduction

Create a dynamic, unforgettable holiday season using a diverse menu of activities and sets for the Advent and Christmas seasons. *Blueprints For Advent And Christmas* contains a collection of congregational tools that evolved over the years in my parish life and always without fail, enhanced the worship experience while delighting and inspiring youth and adults.

The Latin word *liturgia* means "work of the people"; hence, the development and presentation of the sketches and construction of the nativity scenes requires a literal and generous involvement of the "work of the people."

The tools, blueprints, and programmatic scripts invite lay participation especially where the gifts of crafting, acting, and artistry are encouraged and empowered.

Church survey guru, George Barna, estimates that 40% of the typical congregation's members would like to be involved in the life and mission of the church. Chancel dramas and outdoor and indoor nativity scenes that appeal to the visual and dramatic will definitely contribute toward that goal.

Advent Midweek Worship

Advent Midweek Worship Format
With Liturgical Musical Suggestions
Based On "Holden Evening Prayer" By Marty Haugen[1]

Service Of Light
    Procession
    Evening Hymns
    Evening Thanksgiving

Psalmody, Reading, And Canticles
    Silence For Meditation

Lessons

Sketch*

Homily*

The Annunciation

The Magnificat

Litany And Prayers

Final Blessing

Liturgical Musical Suggestions
    Advent 1
        Chant psalm laments in minor key
        Sing Negro spirituals
    Advent 2
        "Mary, Mary, What You Gonna Name That Baby?"
        "Virgin Mary Had A Little Baby"
        "The Magnificat"
    Advent 3
        "Joy To The World" and other carols
    Advent 4
        Typical Christmas carols

---

1. Marty Haugen, "Holden Evening Prayer" available through GIA Publications, 7404 South Mason Avenue, Chicago, Illinois 60638.

* The Sketches and Homilies are about eight minutes each, which is the time between commercials on television and the approximate adult attention span time.

**Advent 1
Sketch**

When Israel Sang The Blues

Characters:
    Jarah
    Eshmore
    Geezer
    Abab
    Stagehand (nonspeaking)

Props:
    Bricks
    Clay
    Salve
    Stringed instrument
    Sign saying "Approximately 714 years later — 586 BCE in Babylon"

**Scene 1
Slavery In Egypt — Longing For A Deliverer!**

Jarah: *(making bricks from clay)* Oh, my aching back!

Eshmore: What's a matter, Jarah, can't you take a little hard work?

Jarah: Makin' bricks in the heat of the day is not my idea of sensible work *or* fun! Living here in Egypt is the pits. I wish we were back home in good, old Canaan.

Eshmore: I know what you mean. My neck is killing me, too. And my hands are dried out by alkaline clay — and look at my face — look at your face! Burned, peeling, ugh.

Jarah: Yeah, and hey, you know what I did?

Eshmore: No, what?

Jarah: I got this salve made from camel's tallow and it really helps. Here, try some.

(Eshmore puts salve on his face and hands and smiles broadly.)

Jarah: And here's the latest. Orders from Pharaoh's goons — we gotta go and find our own straw to put into the bricks for strength. They won't supply it anymore.

Eshmore: Was a lot easier when the Egyptians supplied it.

Jarah: You got that right.

Eshmore: Now I heard that old *(whispers)* Paranoid Pharaoh wants a million bricks for those two towns — Pithom and Ramses.

Jarah: No, really?

Eshmore: Yep, sure as my name is Eshmore Elizer Elbrim.

Jarah: Old Ebenezer collapsed yesterday working out here in the sun.

Eshmore: No wonder. How's he doing?

Jarah: Not good. Heat stroke. Dehydration.

Eshmore: That's one a day for a week.

Jarah: I never thought leaving Canaan and coming to Egypt would end in slavery like this.

Eshmore: Neither did I.

Jarah: You think our God Yahweh has deserted us?

Eshmore: Feels like it.

Jarah: We need a leader to get us out of here — you think there's any hope?

Eshmore: Dunno. I suppose God could do something —☐maybe will.What are you doing, Jarah?

Jarah: *(sits down and plays a stringed instrument)* When I am sad and discouraged, I sing. I sing a sad song. *(hums)* Gotta watch out for Pharaoh's goons, though.

Eshmore: Jarah, your song sounds like a lament.

Jarah: It is.

Eshmore: What are the words?

Jarah: *(strums softly in the background and reads or chants Psalm 22:1-2)* "My God, my God, why have you forsaken me? Why are you so far from helping me, from the words of my groaning?"

Scene 2
Defeated And In Exile — Longing For Hope
(Stagehand carries sign, "Approximately 714 years later — 586 BCE in Babylon.")

Geezer: Here we are in Babylon, Abab, like prisoners with no walls — feels like jail.

Abab: Yes, this so-called exile is no fun.

Geezer: First the Assyrians took over Israel, the northern kingdom — let's see when was that?

Abab: 722 BCE, Geezer.

Geezer: One hundred thirty-six years ago. We thought we were safe here in Judah and in the holy city — Jerusalem.

Abab: We didn't listen to the prophets. We were ripe for the taking and the Babylonians swept over us like a great ocean wave and whisked us away.

Geezer: I wonder, has God deserted us?

Abab: Dunno. What'll we do?

Geezer: Nuttin', I guess — hey, where are you going?

Abab: When I get down, I pick up my instrument and play and sing the blues.

Geezer: The blues?

Abab: Yep. We call them laments.

Geezer: Laments — what are they?

Abab: A Hebrew song that's sad and mad and glad.

Geezer: Sad and mad and glad?

Abab: Yes, here listen. *(chants, sings, or speaks Psalm 137)*

Geezer: That is sad! Makes you feel better though?

Abab: Sure does. Gets my feeling out. I feel a whole lot better now.

Geezer: What else lifts your spirit?

Abab: Hearing what this prophet Isaiah has to say helps, too. Gives me hope.

Geezer: Let's hear it.

Abab: *(reads Isaiah 9:2b)* "The people who walked in darkness have seen a great light; those who lived in a land of deep darkness — on them light has shined."

Geezer: Sounds pretty hopeful. Wonder what that light is or who it is that's coming?

Abab: I wonder, too.

The End

Advent 1
Homily

When Israel Sang The Blues

We've just witnessed a play dramatizing the pain and sadness of the Hebrew people; first as slaves in Egypt before the exodus and then as prisoners in exile.

When Israel lived in dark, bad times like before and during the exodus and during the exile in Babylon, they expressed their sadness by singing. And what did they sing?

They sang the blues. The blues are the laments we find in the book of Psalms, in the book of Lamentations, and in the prophets. Laments, like the blues, are songs that express deep feelings of sadness, disappointment, and yet of hope.

I don't ordinarily sing when I am sad or anxious. The half-Norwegian in me represses feelings quietly and privately.

It's good, though, to listen to, or sing, the blues when one is blue.

When the bandleader, Jimmy Dorsey's, beloved wife died, he sat down and wrote a wonderful lament. You may recognize it.

> *Precious Lord, take my hand, lead me on, let me stand,*
> *I am tired, I am weak, I am worn,*
> *Through the storm, through the night, lead me on to the light,*
> *Take my hand, precious Lord, lead me home.*[1]

How often congregational singing at funerals has brought a lift and a blessing.

One of my favorites is the Blind Boys from Alabama singing that plaintive, lovely spiritual, "Sometimes I Feel Like A Motherless Child."

> *I feel like a motherless chile,*
> *I feel like a motherless chile,*
> *I feel like a motherless chile,*
> *a long, long way from home.*[2]

Oppressed people in every age have been able to identify with those Hebrews who were subjected to slave labor, exile, and refugee status.

African Americans were, and in many cases still are, a people who, while in a strange land, still sing songs to Zion to the glory of God.

The African-American experience in which they groped for meaning, relevance, worth, assurance, reconciliation, civil rights, and a proper response to God, illustrates this common dilemma with the Hebrews in Egypt in exile.

Charles Albert Tindley, pastor of the famous Tindley United Methodist Church in Philadelphia, Pennsylvania, who died in 1933, wrote a lament:

> *I'll overcome some day, I'll overcome some day:*
> *If in my heart I do not yield, I'll overcome some day.*[3]

During the Civil Rights Movement in the '50s and '60s, this lament became the theme song we know as "We Shall Overcome."

We shall overcome, we shall overcome
We shall overcome some day;
Oh, if in our hearts, we do not yield,
We shall overcome some day.[4]

Amnesty International estimates that there are more oppressed people in the world today outside of the communist era than at any time in history. Oppression rears its ugly head in religious fundamentalism, dictatorships, and oppressive regimes. The smog of oppression stains and pains groups of people in all societies.

Oppressed groups may include Native Americans, women, children, gays and lesbians, ethnic clans, and people born into caste systems.

Professor Jim Limburg of Luther Seminary, in his classic paperback, *The Prophets and the Powerless*, reminds us that the powerless are special groups of people in the Old Testament. They are the widows, orphans, poor, and strangers. Isaiah, Amos, and the other prophets denounce the powerful who hold the oppressed down.

A young black convict was heard pleading as he was being executed down South many years ago, "Joe Louis, save me; save me, Joe Louis." Joe Louis, the then heavyweight boxing champion of the world, was this young man's only model of strength, power, and salvation.

The wondrous message of Advent is that God promises a light to come. A deliverer is on the way. "The people who walked in darkness have seen a great light; those who lived in a land of deep darkness — on them the light has shined" (Isaiah 9:2).

Our strength, power, and salvation is coming. Not in a man like Joe Louis, but one who will come in the manner of those oppressed — a poor, simple child.

We continue singing the songs of Advent, the songs of light and hope. Amen.

---

1. "Precious Lord, Take My Hand" words by Thomas A. Dorsey, 1932.

2. "Sometimes I Feel Like A Motherless Chile," African-American spiritual.

3. "We Shall Overcome," African-American spiritual, words by Charles Albert Tindley.

4. *Ibid.*

Advent 2
Sketch

When Maiden Mary Sang The Magnificat

Characters:
　Narrator
　Mary
　Elizabeth
　Zachariah

Props:
　Door
　Gourd

Narrator: They say it was an angel. An angel named Gabriel. Came to Nazareth when the time was right. Stopped by Mary's house. Had a message for Maiden Mary unlike any message ever given. Mary was engaged at this time to a certain Joseph. This Joseph was a distant descendant of King David. The message was astounding. "Greetings, favored one. Don't be afraid. You're going to have a baby and the baby's name will be Yeshuah — Jesus — Son of the Most High God. And your Son will grow up and establish a kingdom that has no end."

　Maiden Mary, shocked and surprised, responded with, "How can this be? Why me?"

　The angel Gabriel persisted and finally Mary submitted and blurted out, "Here I am, the servant of the Lord, let it be with me according to your word."

　Then Mary put on her sandals and her cloak and took off for cousin Elizabeth's house.

Mary: *(knocks, then shouts)* Elizabeth, Elizabeth, it's me — Mary, your favorite cousin from Nazareth. Let me in! Elizabeth, Zachariah, are you home?

Elizabeth: *(opens the door)* Hello, Mary, so good to see you! Come on in. My goodness — you're out of breath — have you been running? Is there a problem?

Mary: Oh, no problem — well, maybe. Hello, sweet Elizabeth. Yes, I've been running. Running, walking, catching rides, and here I am.

Elizabeth: Sit down, dear. Rest. Zach, get some water. Tell me, Mary, what's happening?

Mary: Oh, a most unusual thing happened to me. I had an apparition or maybe it was a dream. Whatever it was — it was real. I, I ...

Elizabeth: *(interrupts)* Go on, Mary, what was it?

Mary: *(takes a drink of water from a gourd Zachariah hands her)* An angel of God came to me ...

Elizabeth: *(interrupt)* An angel?

Mary: Yes, an angel came with this amazing announcement.

Elizabeth: Oh, my. Blessed are you, Mary, blessed among all women — a visit from the almighty.

Mary: This is what happened ...

Elizabeth: *(interrupts)* Before you say any more, something happened to me just when you arrived. You know I am pregnant and the babe in my own womb leaped at the sound of your voice — leaped for joy. Is this the Holy Spirit or what? Go on, Mary.

Mary: Amazing, Elizabeth. Yes, and I, too, am going to have a baby and the baby is of the most high God and he will save us.

Elizabeth: Praise God. But how do you know?

Mary: Remember Hannah?

Elizabeth: Yes.

Mary: Do you remember Hannah's song over Samuel's birth in which God is praised for the salvation of the lowly and oppressed?

Elizabeth: Do I ever! Go on.

Mary: Well, after I received that amazing, unbelievable message, a song came to me, too.

Elizabeth: Say it. Sing it. Let's hear it, if you remember it.

(Mary hums.)

Narrator: And Mary's song began like this: "My soul magnifies the Lord, and my spirit rejoices in God, my Savior, for he has looked with favor on the lowliness of his servant. Surely, from now on all generations will call me blessed: for the Mighty One has done great things for me, and holy is his name ... He has brought down the powerful from their thrones, and lifted up the lowly; he has filled the hungry with good things and sent the rich away empty ..." (Luke 1:47 ff).

After Mary had sung her song, the Magnificat, she stayed three months and then went home. And it came true — generations to the present day call Mary, the mother-to-be blessed!

The End

Advent 2
Homily

When Maiden Mary Sang The Magnificat

Luke 1:39-56 (46-55 — the Magnificat)

We Protestants have not always given Mary, the Mother of Jesus, the honor she deserves. We have felt if we give Mary the praise she deserves, we might appear to be too Roman Catholic. So, we have underplayed her unique and dynamic role in the story of God's salvation.

Surely we have differences in devotion and doctrine about Mary, but tonight Protestants, Catholics, and all Christians must bow in wonder at these incredible events as they unfold.

Softly she sang praises and paraphrases from the Old Testament, forming a wonderful patchwork song — Hebrew textual allusions and images half-borrowed, half-invented from Moses' hymn of praise (Exodus 15:1-18), from Miriam's song (Exodus 15:21), from Asaph (1 Chronicles 16:7-36), from Deborah (Judges 5:1-31), and from David's psalms (Psalm 33; 47; 136).

Mary's song, the Magnificat, gentle in tone, belies its revolutionary content — so revolutionary that it has been banned in dictatorships in Africa and South America.

The Magnificat is a song of freedom and liberation.

> *He has brought down the powerful from their thrones, and lifted up the needy, He has filled the hungry with good things, and sent the rich away empty.* — Luke 1:52-53

This is a ballad about revolution. From the barrios to the balconies of the rich, this is good news to the poor and not-so-good news for the privileged. God turns all things upside down. God brings in a new order, a new vision, and a new hope, "Behold, I make all things new."

Mary is pregnant. Can you see her sitting and rocking at Elizabeth and Zachariah's house? Cousins have just shared intimate, miraculous secrets that will change the world. Old Elizabeth condemned to barrenness is about to have a child and the virgin maiden Mary is expecting, too. Little did either cousin know that both children, second cousins, would meet violent deaths — one by decapitation and the other by crucifixion.

Mary begins by humming softly. In the animal world, did you know that llamas hum? When a llama mama is pregnant and she's going to have a baby, she starts humming. Even after the baby llama is born, the mama llama keeps on humming. She hums throughout her baby's infancy. It's only when the baby llama starts growing up and getting bigger that the mama llama stops humming. Why does she hum? What song is she humming? We don't know. We just know that before the baby is born she hums.

Mary is surprised and so happy that she breaks out in a song to God. She sings, "My soul magnifies the Lord" — the Magnificat, a song of praise, a song of freedom and liberation, and a song that one day will provide life and energy for all. "My soul magnifies the Lord, and my spirit rejoices in God my Savior" (Luke 1:46).

Soon Mary would see the child of God sleep in a feeding trough. Soon she would hear of the angels who sang in the heavens. Then Mary, though perplexed at times, would watch this young man grow up and mature and teach and heal. One day, on a dark Friday, she would see her son suffer and die. Not aware of all this, Mary launches into a song that praises the mighty one whose name is holy.

Then Mary sings:

> *He [God] has helped his servant Israel, in remembrance of his mercy, according to the promise he made to our ancestors, to Abraham and to his descendants forever.* — Luke 1:54-55

Rooted in past promises, Mary sings of a future that fills all believers with confidence and hope. That future is ours tonight because we are freed from sin, death, and the power of the devil.

Two pregnant women tonight — one the mother of John the Baptist, the other the mother of the Savior of the world.

To be pregnant is to be filled with new life, new possibilities, and a new future. Amen.

**Advent 3
Sketch**

Joy To The World

Characters:
 Reporter
 Issac

Props:
 Notebook
 Pen/pencil

Reporter: Here I am in Southampton, England — a reporter for the local *Gazette* and I have to find a story for tomorrow morning's paper. Everybody is so busy Christmas shopping — they look like they don't want to be bothered with an interview. *(paces nervously)* Oh, what am I going to do?

 Oh, here is a young fellow who I believe I'll try. Hmmm, I do know him. His father is in prison and I did a story on that last year. I'll interview him and see if I can come up with a newsworthy story.

 Ah, hello there, ah, Mr. Watts.

Issac: Hello yourself. You know me?

Reporter: Why, yes, ah, er, your father was in the news ...

Issac: *(interrupts)* I don't want to talk about it — good-bye.

Reporter: No, no, we all know your father was in prison for a good reason. Many of us know he was a dissenter for his religious views and really unjustly jailed.

Issac: You're not doing an exposé, are you?

Reporter: No, no — I want to interview *you* — they say as a small boy you amused your parents by writing rhymes.

Issac: *(visibly relieved at the subject)* That I did.

Reporter: They say you showed the signs of poetic genius and ...

Issac: *(interrupts)* I don't know about that. It is true I wrote hymns for worship at church.

Reporter: Tell me about that. How did you happen to write hymns? I hear *great* hymns that are becoming so popular. *(writes in his notebook as Issac speaks)*

Issac: To be frank, I got really impatient with those wretched paraphrases of the psalms they sang in all the churches here in England and in Scotland.

Reporter: They are rather dull — I quit the church, at least in part, because they are so archaic and tedious.

Issac: Oh, you did?

Reporter: Yes! "Scandalous doggerel" Samuel Wesley, father of the Wesley boys, called 'em. So what got you going on writing hymns, Mr. Issac Watts? *(continues taking notes)*

Issac: Well, I publicly objected to the psalm-singing in my father's church in Southampton and one of the church elders heard me complain and shot back at me, "Give me something better, young man!"

Reporter: And how old were you?

Issac: Only eighteen.

Reporter: What did you do?

Issac: I wrote a hymn that very Sunday — and the congregation loved it — so I kept on writing more and more and more.

Reporter: How many in all?

Issac: Two hundred ten.

Reporter: Two hundred ten? Why, that's amazing!

Issac: I loved doing it.

Reporter: Name some of your hymns.

Issac: *(scratches his head)* Let's see. "When I Survey The Wondrous Cross" and "Jesus Shall Reign," just to name a couple.

Reporter: What hymn did you write that is the most loved and sung of all?

Issac: Without a doubt — "Joy To The World"!

Reporter: You wrote "Joy To The World"? Why, that's my favorite — even though I dropped out of church some time ago.

Issac: Mine, too. Say, Mr. (Ms.) Reporter, maybe you'd like to come back to church — you'll enjoy the singing, I'm sure. Say, instead of just inviting you back, I'll pick you up next Sunday in my carriage. Okay?

Reporter: Well, ah, thank you for the interview, Issac Watts — about church, we'll see.

Issac: You're welcome — hope to see you Sunday.

The End

**Advent 3
Homily**

When Teddy Roosevelt Sang Bass

Two seminary presidents, David Tiede and the late Timothy Lull, introduced their Advent devotional, *Let Heaven and Nature Sing*, with a fascinating story about Teddy Roosevelt. President Teddy Roosevelt was famous for his enthusiasm and gusto in life. He once hoped the heavenly choir would include 10,000 sopranos, 10,000 altos, 10,000 tenors, and he would sing bass! The first hymn he may have had in mind for the chorus would be "Joy To The World," so he could belt out the resounding bass line, "And heaven and nature sing!"

Teddy Roosevelt brought joy to the earth! He loved the open skies and the endless prairies on his ranch in Medora, North Dakota. He loved his work of conservation of natural resources. He was a steward of the earth.

When one looks up at that spectacled and mustached figure on Mount Rushmore, one can imagine a twinkle in his eyes and a smile on his lips as he looks out over the Black Elk National Forest, the vast public forest land and beautiful Black Hills kept in protective custody for generations to come.

Teddy loved and brought joy to the earth by his vision, his passion, and his firm convictions.

It's the same spirit of gusto and enthusiasm you and I feel in these four weeks of Advent — let heaven and nature sing! The psalmist sings, "Let the floods clap their hands, let the hills sing together for joy at the presence of the Lord, for he is coming to judge the earth" (Psalm 98:8).

The prophet Isaiah prophesies, "For you shall go out in joy, and be led in peace; the mountains and the hills before you shall burst into song and all the trees of the field shall clap their hands" (Isaiah 55:12).

Can you imagine the golden aspens in the Black Hills clapping their hands? Can you imagine the ponderosa pines, the cottonwoods, and the willows along the Mississippi clapping their hands in unrestrained joy?

What an image! No wonder. Someone is coming! Someone whose wounded hand rests on our shoulders. We're already to sing. Joy to the earth! Joy to the world! Joy to the cosmos! Joy to the universe! Let heaven and nature sing!

One of the most famous expressions of joy comes from French philosopher and mathematician, Blaise Pascal.

> *In the year of grace 1654, Monday 23 November ... from about half-past ten in the evening till about half an hour after midnight: FIRE ... God of Abraham, God of Isaac, God of Jacob. Not of the philosophers and the learned. Certitude. Certitude. Emotion. Joy ... Joy! Joy! Joy! Tears of Joy ... my God ... Let me not be separated from thee for ever.*[1]

Pascal carried this description of his experience with him for the rest of his life.

Can you recall a time when you broke out in laughter ... in unrestrained joy? A gift unexpected at Christmas or a good word from the doctor on your diagnosis? I remember my wife walking out of the doctor's office in Yankton, South Dakota, with a smile on her face — yes, we were going to have our first baby.

Now is the season of unrestrained joy. Surely, Christmas time is, for many, the loneliest time of the year, when family tensions are high and guilt over past sins and resentments are floating to the surface.

It can be a time about a lady trampled in a buying frenzy at a Wal-Mart superstore. Hopefully, Christmas is more about generosity, love, forgiveness, and laughter.

Let's build a house of Laughter,
Where joy sounds from every rafter.
All could there extol
Joy's good for the soul!
For saints here and in the hereafter.[2]

Our joy is more permanent and longer lasting than the whoops, hollers, and smiles when Saddam Hussein was captured.

One day, I got this card in the mail from Saint Martin, Guadaloupe. It depicted a beautiful Dutch West Indies sunset. It was from Neil Kittleson, whose lovely wife had died and I had conducted the funeral. Neil then moved away to Minneapolis. There he met a lady named Bobbie and they married. All Neil wrote was, "Yippee! Yippee! Yippee! Neil and Bobbie."

Sing, heavenly choirs — all 10,000 sopranos, 10,000 altos, 10,000 tenors, and Teddy Roosevelt singing bass. And heaven and nature sing! Sing, sing, sing, joy to the world — God has come. Amen.

---

1. Blaise Pascal (1623-1662) http://www.burgy.50megs.com/blaise.htm.

2. Cal and Rose Samra, *Rolling In The Aisles (The Holy Humor Series)* (Colorado Springs: WaterBrook Press, 1999).

Mini-Dramas For Cycles A And B

Synopses Of The Mini-Dramas For Cycle A

Whose Birthday Is It Anyway?
Jason experiences a very strange birthday. He is frustrated by the turn of events in the Land of Puzzling Tales. A better way to celebrate his birthday is suggested.

Philippe
This "morality poem" is about a young lad who would rather *sleep* than get involved in life. He meets up with a wolf who threatens him and then eats him and when disgorged realizes the necessary change that must be made in his life.

Gummy Old Men
Two elderly men meet and reminisce about their earlier life together. They share little anecdotes — proudly at first. Then the telling of stories becomes tainted with remorse and regrets. They decide to do something positive about the past.

The Water Witcher
A grandfather and grandson are painting a tool shed on a hobby farm. The grandfather tells the grandson about the mysterious way in which water was discovered on the farm. A skeptic neighbor does not believe in "water witching." The grandson is confronted with the choice of believing his grandfather or the neighbor as he drinks a cold, refreshing glass of water from the old well.

No Clues?
A somewhat bumbling detective talks with his pregnant wife about a recent crime he has successfully solved. Meanwhile, the wife hints about her condition (she is pregnant with triplets), of which he is completely unaware. In the end, the detective thinks they're getting a new puppy.

Looking For The Child Of Bethlehem
Asher, the son of an innkeeper in Bethlehem, tells of the birth of Jesus, and then visits with contemporary shoppers and carolers in a quest to find out about the meaning of Jesus' coming. Asher discovers, in the end, that Jesus is the promised Messiah and invites all to praise God.

Where's Dad?
A 21-year-old young man plans to meet his father in order to confront him about his feelings of emotional abandonment. The father doesn't show up and the young man shares his frustrations and feelings of abandonment to a total stranger. In the end, the audience is led to believe that the father is at long last breaking the pattern by showing up after all. Preaching themes may focus on Joseph as a fatherly model.

The Difference Between Getting And Giving
An old man, at the end of his life, ponders the difference between getting and giving. He talks to several people who have interacted with him in life but is unable to get a satisfactory answer. Finally, he talks to the Lord in heaven and the audience is left to fill in the answer.

Prepare: An Advent Play
Santa Claus plays opposite John the Baptist in this play about the meaning of Advent in which the two characters articulate messages that compete for our attention prior to Christmas.

General Advent Sketch
Cycle A

Whose Birthday Is It Anyway?

Theme: An alternative way to celebrate Christmas

Characters:
- Narrator
- Jason
- Children (nonspeaking)
- Father
- Son
- Daughter
- Mother
- Player 1
- Player 2
- Mr. Brown
- Grandmother
- Mrs. Brown
- Letter Carrier

Props:
- Basket
- Ball
- Table and chairs
- Eating utensils
- A-1 Sauce bottle
- Door
- Cake
- Packages
- Mail bag
- Cards
- Unicycle or bicycle
- Megaphone

(Music plays in the background.)

Narrator: This is a story about Jason, an eight-year-old boy who had a very strange birthday celebration.

(Jason walks to center stage.)

Narrator: Jason lived in the Land of Puzzling Tales. In this land, the unexpected always happened, and Jason's neighborhood was no exception.

(Jason joins other children.)

Narrator: The children in this land played kneeball instead of football. They played basketball by throwing a basket over a ball, instead of throwing the ball into a basket.

(Children throw a basket over a ball, laugh, giggle, and have a good time. Scene fades.)

Narrator: The people in this strange land ate steak for breakfast and oatmeal for supper.

(A family seated at a table, frozen until this point, begin to eat and speak.)

Father: Good morning, family. Pass the steak and mashed potatoes. I love A-1 Sauce early in the morning.

Son: Me, too, Dad. Pass the onions.

Daughter: What's for supper, Mom?

Mother: I'm preparing some cheerios with all the 1% milk you can drink. How does that sound?

Father: Oatmeal or cheerios for supper is fine — as long as I get a little yogurt with it.

(Scene fades.)

Narrator: Everyone in this strange land mowed their lawns in winter and shoveled snow in the summer. They *laughed* at sad stories.

Player 1: Did you hear about Lassie, our neighbor's dog? Beautiful collie. She was guiding a blind man across the street over by Belgrade Avenue when she was struck and killed by a city maintenance truck. Happened just last week.

(Players laugh as scene fades.)

Narrator: And they *cried* at funny stories.

Player 2: A man owned a mouse that could talk, sing, and play the piano. One day he put the mouse up for sale along with a talking bird for $10,000. A buyer came. The owner agreed to sell the two together. When the deal was done, the original owner said, "I sure tricked him. That bird couldn't talk, it was only a ventriloquist mouse."

(Players cry as scene fades.)

Narrator: All in all, it was a strange sort of place. Now on Jason's birthday, as usual, the unusual happened. Jason's grandparents came from their home across the state to visit and help celebrate. When they arrived in Jason's neighborhood, they went immediately to the Browns' house, down the street, and stayed there for the day.

(Older couple approach a door and knock or ring the doorbell.)

Mr. Brown: Sounds like someone's at the door, Lucy. *(opens door)* Well, hello. May I help you?

Grandmother: Oh, hello. We are Jason's grandparents and we came to town and thought we would celebrate Jason's birthday with you — even though you don't know him.

Mrs. Brown: Oh, yes, I'm sure we can get acquainted — come right in. It'll be fun to get to know you and celebrate with you.

(Scene fades.)

Narrator: Jason's mother baked a birthday cake, of course, but she gave it to the letter carrier to eat when he arrived with the mail that day.

Letter Carrier: Here's your mail, ma'am. Why, what's this? *(takes cake from Mother)*

Mother: It's cake, of course, for our birthday celebration.

Letter Carrier: Thanks! It looks delicious. I'll eat it and if there's anything left over, I'll feed my cocker spaniel.

(Scene fades.)

Narrator: When the neighborhood children heard about Jason's birthday, they exchanged gifts with one another, but, of course, Jason got none.

(Children exchange packages. Jason holds out his hands, then drops them in disappointment.)

Narrator: Then the whole bunch went out "Happy Birthdaying" through the streets, singing Happy Birthday to all the neighbors.

(Children sing one verse of the song using "dear neighbors.")

Narrator: There was a blizzard of birthday cards.

(Letter Carrier opens his mail bag and hands out the cards.)

Narrator: The post office had to hire extra workers and work longer hours to handle the deluge of cards. Of course, in the Land of Puzzling Tales, the expected was the unexpected, and all the children, moms, dads, grandparents, and even a couple of dogs and a parakeet got cards, while poor Jason got none.

(Players pass cards back and forth, throwing them into the air while dancing around.)

Narrator: Jason went down the street, borrowed the school cheerleaders' megaphone, jumped on his unicycle, and rode up and down the street shouting.

Jason: *(loudly, through megaphone)* Whose birthday is it anyway?

All Players: *(chant softly, and increase the volume with each line)*
Whose birthday is it anyway?
Whose birthday is it anyway?
Whose birthday is it anyway?

(Scene fades.)

Optional Ending 1

Read an Advent scripture and/or sing an Advent hymn or a Christmas carol.

Optional Ending 2

Narrator: The baby Jesus will be kidnapped again this year and held for a ransom of millions of dollars. This year Americans will surrender about twenty billion dollars to the stores to buy gifts to swap. But it is Jesus' birthday! Jesus ought to receive the gifts. Jesus said, "Inasmuch as you have done it to the least of these my brethren you have done it to me" (Matthew 25:40). We give to Jesus when we give to the poor, the weak, the hungry, the homeless, the refugees, and the prisoners. It will be a great birthday celebration when God's people begin in earnest to give once again to Jesus. For after all, it is his birthday, isn't it?

The End

**Advent 1
Cycle A**

Philippe

Texts: Isaiah 2:1-5; Psalm 122; Romans 13:11-14; Matthew 24:36-44

Theme: Better to be awake and alert than apathetic and asleep

Characters:
  Philippe (lazy)
  Mother (concerned)
  Father (disciplinarian)
  Wolf
  White Cross rescue workers

Tone: Cynical, instructive

Setting/Props: "Philippe" may be read with or without actors. The congregation may be invited to be a part of a children's time as this play sets up the context for effective preaching in the sermon on the theme of being ready for the coming Messiah.

Suggested song: "Wake up, Sleeper, Arise," by Handt Hanson, © Prince of Peace Publishing, licensed by CCLI

Approximate time: 5 minutes

There once was a lad
named Philippe (fil—leep)
who would only say,
"I'd rather sleep!"
Hear his story now my friend,
for an amazing moral
lies at the end.

Scene 1

One day
his mother said
when Philippe
fell out of bed,
"Good Morning,
my darling boy

you are my pride and joy."
Philippe said,
"I'd rather sleep."

"What would you like to eat?"
"I'd rather sleep."
"Some tasty
cream of wheat?"
"I'd rather sleep."
"My child, didn't you hear
the clock go beep?"
"I'd rather sleep."
"Or feel me tickle
both your feet?"
"I'd rather sleep."

"You must listen
when I call."
"I'd rather sleep."
"It's time to fly
up to the mall."
"I'd rather sleep."
"Don't you want
to come, my dear?"
"I'd rather sleep!"
"Oh, you'd rather
stay right here?"
"I'd rather sleep."

So Mom went
to the mall and
let Philippe sleep.

Scene 2

His father said,
"shut off the screen,
that's just what I mean."
Philippe said,
"I'd rather sleep."
"Couch potato
that you are —"
"I'd rather sleep."
"— with your studies
you'll not get far!"
"I'd rather sleep."

"If you lie
horizontal still —"
"I'd rather sleep."
"— we'll never, ever
get up the hill!"
"I'd rather sleep."
"If only you would
say, 'No doze for me.' "
"I'd rather sleep."
"A vacation we could take
Mom and me, we three."
"I'd rather sleep."

So Mom and Dad
left Philippe.
They let him sleep.

Scene 3

Now as Philippe
began to nap,
as in a dream, at the door
did someone rap.
"Come in, come in,"
Philippe did say.
"What's mine is yours — you may."
"Your life," said the wolf
who entered now,
"no cow, no sow, you bow."
"I'd rather sleep."

**"I am hungry can't
you see?"**
"I'd rather sleep."
**"I will eat you
count to three."**
"I'd rather sleep."
**"Okay, snoring snot,
in my belly you will rot!"**
"I'd rather sleep."

**"Do you want
to say good-bye?"**
"I'd rather sleep."
**"To Mom, to Dad,
to all on high."**
"I'd rather sleep."

So the Wolf
ate Philippe!

Scene 4

1. Arriving home
   at 8 o'clock,
   his parents had
   a dreadful shock!
   They found a Wolf
   upon the floor
   sleeping like he'd
   never slept before.
   Through sleepy lids
   the Wolf did say,
   **"I'd rather sleep
   all day today."**

   They grabbed the Wolf
   by his legs.
   They made him swallow
   forty eggs.
   "Cough up Philippe,"
   his mother yelled.
   The Wolf replied,
   "I'd rather sleep."
   "Oh no," his father cried,
   "Philippe he will not keep."

Scene 5

Meanwhile,
inside the Wolf, Philippe
did dial,
911 while avoiding
stomach bile.
Cellular phones,
they are the best
especially in wolves
who are not at rest.

White Cross they did come,
and shook the Wolf — the bum.
Until he woke and
gave a roar
and Philippe fell out
upon the floor.

He rubbed his eyes
and scratched his head,
He was so glad
because he wasn't dead.
And Mom and Dad gave him a hug,
as he sat upon the rug.

His mother said
to her darling boy,
"How are you doing my
pride and joy?"
"I am feeling better,
sweet mother dear,
I want to write a letter
to this hemisphere,
And this is what I'll say,
'I'd rather stay
awake, not sleep,
for goodness sake!
Alive, alert,
and ready.'"

The Wolf chimed in,
"So that is what you plan to do —
then may I your friend be, too?"
The Wolf moved into
the guest house,
and they all lived
somewhat happily
ever after.

The Moral of Philippe:
Stay Awake
Stay Alert
Be Alive!

                                                    The End

Advent 2
Cycle A

Gummy Old Men

Texts: Isaiah 11:1-10; Psalm 72:1-7, 18-19; Romans 15:4-13; Matthew 3:1-12

Theme: Reflection, remorse, repentance, renewal

Characters:
 Norb (older man)
 Earl (older man)

Tone: Humorous, serious, sad, hopeful

Setting/Props: Bench in a city park near the retirement home

Approximate time: 5-7 minutes

(Musical introduction)

Norb: Well, for goodness sake, if it isn't me ole friend, Earl. When did they let you out?

Earl: Hiya, Norb. They always let us out — right after coffee. "Feed the monkeys, chase 'em out." You know how retirement homes work. Haven't seen ya fer a while Norb — where ya been?

Norb: Been to see my daughter in Texas. Had to get out of my apartment for a break. Lula, that's my second daughter, called me one day and said, "Come on down, Dad, see the grandkids. Play some shuffleboard. Get bored out of your ever loving mind." So I went. Been there a month. Glad to be gone, glad to be back.

Earl: Like your apartment?

Norb: It's small, but it's okay. Not like your own home, you know.

Earl: Yeah, I gave mine up now almost four years ago. Moved here to the zoo. That's the way it seems sometimes. You know, Norb, I'll be 78 next week.

Norb: No kidding. Well I'm right behind you, Earl, I'll be 76 my next birthday. *(pauses, then says nostalgically)* Remember when we farmed in Lexington County?

Earl: You bet. Good old days. We must have run 2,000 acres between us.

Norb: There wasn't a nicer spread than your farm and mine. Remember County Extension Agent O'Connell? He always bragged us up. We got along real well in those days.

Earl: Remember when we got picked to do those experimental plots for the University? *(laughs)* Didn't pay much but we sure learned a lot about hybrid seed corn.

Norb: That's fer shur.

Earl: And you know, I think that highfalutin' college prof learned a few things, too.

Norb: What a young fool!

Norb: Our kids did okay at the state fair, too. Imagine seven purple ribbons one year. And your kids got several that year, too, didn't they?

Earl: Yeah. Couple of purple and a slew of blues. We had Delilah, that Guernsey heifer that year.

Norb: I remember her.

Earl: She was a class act. So was the champion lamb. Hated to sell her.

Norb: Good times, eh, Earl?

Earl: Yeah ... but ...

Norb: But what?

Earl: Oh, nothin'.

Norb: What do you mean — nothin'? *(pauses)* Spit it out, Earl! We're either satisfied and proud of our achievements or we're not.

Earl: Well, it's not that simple.

Norb: What isn't that simple?

Earl: You know ...

Norb: You know? What in the sam hill are you getting at?

Earl: Well —

Norb: You got regrets. Oh fine.

Earl: No, not really.

Norb: Oh — I see it —

Earl: No, you don't see it.

Norb: Oh yes, I do, you sound downright remorseful.

Earl: So?

Norb: So?

Earl: *(blurts out)* It's one thing to get somewhere in life and do it with a clean conscience, but, Norb, how do you think we got where we got?

Norb: Good hard work.

Earl: — 2,000 acres of the best farmland in Lexington County?

Norb: You bet!

Earl: — rolling hills, creek adjacent to your farm and mine?

Norb: Always liked that creek ...

Earl: I've been thinking lately ...

Norb: Thinking? You've been *brooding* —

Earl: Face it, Norb. We got what we got on the backs of our neighbors who didn't make it.

(Norb shrugs his shoulders.)

Earl: Remember the auction?

Norb: Auction, bauction! *(angrily)*

Earl: Now you listen to me, Norb — when they sold Henry Lawrenson's place, all of us neighbors agreed to block the auction.

Norb: Yeah.

Earl: We all wore red bandanas in solidarity with Henry and Lucille.

Norb: I remember.

Earl: But who went against the agreement? You and me Norb, we bid on Henry's farm and we *got* it!

Norb: Someone had to buy it.

Earl: Legally, sure! But morally? I wonder....

Norb: So that's what's bugging you after all these years? Sounds like we'd better talk about it and deal with it. I know, I know what we did.

Earl: And listen with both ears, Norb, that's not all. And this has nothing to do with you — it's my issue but I've been thinking about how I treated our school superintendant Milo Dariman. I was with that gang who got him ousted. I just got caught up in the emotion of it all — they wanted to raise taxes.

Norb: They were too high already.

Earl: — build a new addition —

Norb: — didn't need that —

Earl: — raise the teachers' salaries —

Norb: — they were too high already —

Earl: — add a music and drama coach —

Norb: — foolish —

Earl: — seemed outlandish at the time — but now lookin' at it from the long view, I've been thinkin' ...

Norb: Well, Earl, I admit I was with *that* group, too, you know — that's quite a few years ago now. I know we were wrong and we behaved badly. We actually believed some of those crazy rumors, passed them on and got all bent out of shape — we really smeared his name. I wonder if Superintendent Dariman ever got over it. You know he got sick after we kicked him out. Mmmmm. *(pauses)*

Earl: Dunno, Norb. Some things, maybe we just got to forget.

Norb: No, Earl, you're right in bringing this up. I don't think we should just forget this. All this is buggin' us fer a reason. Some things we need to admit and get it out and if possible fix it.

Earl: Yeah, Norb, that's what I'm feeling.

Norb: Let's see, I wonder if Henry is still in Texas ... and Superintendant Dariman is still at that new school. I'll bet I could call him in Centerville or maybe the both of us could write him a note and ...

(Music plays as lights fade out.)

The End

**Advent 3
Cycle A**

The Water Witcher

Texts: Isaiah 35:1-10; Psalm 146:4-9 or Luke 1:47-55; James 5:7-10; Matthew 11:2-11

Theme: Difficulty of believing and the possiblity of doubt turned into faith

Characters:
  Grandfather Willard Adamson
  Grandson Joey (eleven years old or younger)
  Slick (skeptic neighbor)

Tone: Nurturing relationship, encouragement

Setting/Props:
  Imaginary tool shed
  Paintbrushes
  Paint
  Imaginary old-fashioned well pump
  Cup
  Y-shaped stick
  One option that may enhance the scene would be an actual old-fashioned well pump. There are still a few of these around on abandoned farms, museums, and as decorative objects for flower gardens.

Approximate time: 7-8 minutes

Grandpa Willard: Okay, Joey, we'll paint this tool shed first and then the other buildings. Have you ever painted before?

Joey: Only my mother's wallpaper when she wasn't lookin'.

Willard: *(laughs)* Ho, ho. How about for real?

Joey: Not really, Grandpa. It looks like fun. Where's my brush?

Willard: There it is, Joey. You can use the brush that is in the can of linseed oil.

Joey: How come it's in there?

Willard: To keep it pliable and soft. Now dip your brush carefully and away you go.

Joey: How long will it take, Grandpa?

Willard: A couple of hours.

Joey: Whew, that's a long time.

Willard: When you're tired, Joey, just take a break. We'll pump some water from the well over there and get a drink when you're thirsty. Grandma sent along some chocolate chip cookies.

(They paint in silence for a while.)

Willard: Let's play a game, Joey.

Joey: Okay, what'll it be?

Willard: Let me tell you a story. You guess if it is fact or fib.

Joey: I love your stories, Grandpa, but I'm never sure if you're making them up or they are real.

Willard: *(laughs)* Once upon a time there were two jokers.

Joey: Like in cards?

Willard: No, just two friendly guys that liked each other. They went fishing together, went to McDonald's and had a strawberry shake, went to baseball games together, and saw the Twins play a couple of times every summer. These two guys made slingshots out of "Y" tree branches and they took willow sticks and threw mud balls ... Then one day an old grinch came along and interrupted their play and said, "Hey you two joker loafers, it's time to get some work done...."

Joey: Oh, Grandpa, you're talking about us, you and me. That's an easy fact or fib story. It's true.

Willard: Yep, you're right.

Joey: I'm thirsty.

Willard: Already?

Joey: Yep, hungry, too. I think I smell chocolate chip cookies.

Willard: *(laughs)* Okay, let's go to the pump and get a drink.

Joey: Can I pump?

Willard: Sure, lad, just take a long, steady stroke.

(Joey pumps and Willard holds a cup — they drink and smile.)

Willard: How is it? Like its taste?

Joey: Ohhh — it's cold and delicious! Not like town water with chemicals and all.

Willard: It's pure. No pollution. Natural, right from the aquifer 'bout a hundred feet down.

Joey: Wow. What's an aquifer?

Willard: Like an underground lake.

Joey: *(puzzled)* Well, how did they ever find the water so they could drill the well?

Willard: Well ...

Joey: Now, Grandpa, is this one of those fact or fib stories?

Willard: Well, maybe 'tis and maybe 'tisn't. Remember when we saw old Bill Bardigen out in the grove of trees yesterday?

Joey: Yeah, Grandpa, and he had this strange stick in his hand and seemed busy at somethin'. Didn't even wave back at us.

Willard: Wasn't a stick. It was a willow branch and he was witching for water.

Joey: Witching for water? What's that?

Willard: Well, certain people have this gift to be able to find water. They take a branch like this "Y" or a metal crow bar or a pair of pliers and walk along until it moves the divining tool.

Joey: Oh, Grandpa ... fib, fib, fib.

Willard: No, Joey, I know it's hard to believe but it's true. I've seem Bill Bardigen do it right here on my acreage. The willow branch twists right out of his hand with such an unseen power and a force so strong that you couldn't resist it if you wanted to. Points right to where the water is. I've tried it myself but it don't work. But it does for him.

Joey: Wow, you mean it always works for Bill?

Willard: Yep, never fails.

Joey: That's like magic.

Willard: It's more than magic — it's a mystery of nature — only God knows the secret. Oh, here comes Slick, my neighbor to the north.

Slick: Heya, how are you doing, Willard?

Willard and Joey: *(together)* Great — you?

Slick: Awful! My tractor broke down, my wife is sick, and my dog ran away.

Willard: Well, it could be worse, Slick, your dog could be sick and your wife could have run away. *(laughs)*

Slick: *(laughs, brightens up a bit)* I suppose so ...

Joey: Hey, Mr. Slick, Grandpa and I've been talkin' about this well where we got a drink a bit ago.

Slick: Yeah, so what?

Joey: Grandpa said a water witcher found this well.

Slick: Ha, ha, your grandpa's filling you with that malarky?

Joey: *(defensively)* Well it's true — isn't it, Grandpa?

Willard: *(nods)* Seen it many times, Slick. They call those who can do it, dowsers, they use a diviner's rod ...

Slick: *(retorts)* No way, José! I don't believe it. It's pure coincidence. What are you, a weirdo? What's the big idea, Willard, filling your grandson with stuff like that?

Willard: *(ticked off)* Well see here, tricky slicky, since when do you know so much?

Joey: Yeah. Grandpa said old Bill Bardigen just took a willow stick and walked around the farm and right here at this spot it twisted down like magic — they dug a hole and voilà — water!

Slick: Ho, ho, you fools! It's all fantasy. I read all about "water witching" in Nevill Drury's book the *Dictionary of Mysticism and the Occult*. They say the witching rod resembles the implement witches ride on on their black sabbaths — all hooey, baloney. Your Mr. Bill Bardigen is a fake. I don't believe in nothing I can't see with my eyes and fix with these two hands.

Willard: But, but, Slick, I'm not saying "witching water" is witchery and black magic and dabbling in the occult, I just ...

Slick: *(interrupts)* I'll hear no more of your prattle, Mr. Willard Adamson — you should know better — see you around.

Joey: But ... it's true ... Grandpa said so ...

Slick: I don't believe in anything I can't understand, touch, or see — so there. *(exits)*

(Grandpa and Joey go back to painting silently.)

Joey: It is true isn't it, Grandpa?

(Willard remains silent.)

Joey: Water witching and all that?

Willard: *(looks at Joey, puts down paintbrush, goes over to the pump and pumps a glass of water, smiles, drinks, smiles, drinks again)* It's good water, isn't it Joey?

Joey: Sure is. *(smiles and drinks, too, then nods head knowingly)* I get it. I get it.

The End

**Advent 4
Cycle A**

No Clues?

Texts: Isaiah 7:10-16; Psalm 80:1-7, 16-18; Romans 1:1-7; Matthew 1:18-25

Theme: See the signs — they're very clear

Characters:
    Detective Joe Clue
    Damis (Joe's pregnant wife)

Tone: Humorous

Setting/Props:
    Kitchen table
    Flowers in a vase
    Two or three chairs
    Coffee pot
    Radio
    Knitting needles
    Yarn
    Couch
    Baby clothes

Approximate time: 5 minutes

Damis: *(talking to herself)* Ooooh. Morning comes too soon. I'll fix myself some coffee. Maybe some java will wake me up and get me going. I think I'll fix myself a little cream of wheat, too. Maybe it'll settle my touchy stomach — ooooh. *(holds stomach)* Guess I'll make some coffee for Joe, too. Heard on the police scanner last night that he investigated that homicide at Ringo's Bar. Wonder what happened? So much violence nowadays. I worry about Joe. But he's good. Loves his work. So focused. *(looks offstage)* Say, Joe, hon, are you getting up, or are you sleeping in?

Joe: *(sleepily from offstage)* Yeah. dear, I'm getting up — I'll be right out — make some coffee will you?

Damis: Coffee! 10-4. *(turns on radio — soft music begins playing)*

Joe: *(appears looking a bit tusseled)* Morning, love. *(kisses Damis)*

Damis: Here's your Norwegian gasoline, my Latin lover. High octane.

Joe: Thanks, Damis. Man — what a night. What a night! *(unaware of Damis' discomfort)*

Damis: You and me both.

Joe: Got over to Ringo's Bar as soon as I heard the call. Did you hear it over the scanner, Damis?

Damis: I did but what happened?

Joe: Well, I been trying to piece the evidence together — the bartender was killed last night about 10:05 p.m. with a blunt instrument — perhaps a broom handle.

Damis: A broom handle? Hardly a deadly weapon.

Joe: Yeah, or maybe it was a mop stick.

Damis: Do you know who did it?

Joe: I'm getting to it. Who do *you* think? A patron, the janitor, maybe the bartender's deranged brother-in-law? *(pauses)* What's the matter, hon?

Damis: I'm not feeling good, Joe. Every morning, it seems — just not feeling right.

Joe: Probably a touch of the flu — something going around. Here, I'll get some Pepto-Bismol®. Good for a queasy stomach. Got a bottle in my squad car — I take it whenever I get a messy case to solve and when the stress level gets a few degrees too high.

Damis: No, no, I'm fine. I'll just lie down and eat this cream of wheat.

Joe: *(continues with his story)* ... So I got to the bar and there was old Manfred lying face down on the floor in a puddle of blood. Coroner said he had suffered a fierce blow to the head. It caved in his skull — must have done him in instantly.

Damis: Oh, ugly ... poor Manfred. Didn't get to enjoy much of his retirement did he?

Joe: Nope. Officer Olson showed me the key clue!

Damis: Well, detective Joe, what was the *key* clue?

Joe: You'll never guess. And it led right to the suspect.

Damis: Well, tell me, what was it?

Joe: All that training in the police academy and my years of experience on the beat and now two years in the detective department paid off.

Damis: Sherlock Holmes, what was it? *(as Damis questions Joe she is knitting some little booties, and from time to time rubs her abdomen as if in pain — Joe doesn't notice her grimace)*

Joe: Sick every morning, eh? Could be something you ate. Well, anyway....

Damis: Yes, yes, go on .... *(sits down wearily)*

Joe: I examined the bloody mop stick, found no fingerprints on it. Then I detected a book of matches on the floor — which apparently had fallen out of the assailant's pocket. I picked it up with my tweezers and noted that it was a matchbook from Pepper's Bar and Lounge from across the street. Then it rang a bell. Louie Pepper hated Ralph Ringo. They competed against each other for years. And besides that, Louie was Ralph's brother-in-law. It all fit together. They've hated each other for all these years, got into an argument last night and whamo....

Damis: What happened then? Oh, Joe, honey, I think I'll lie down for a bit. *(lays down)* Okay, that feels better. Here take these little booties I'm knitting and put them on the chest of drawers.

Joe: Officer Petrice and I went over to Louie Pepper's and sure enough, he looked like he'd been in a fight — bloodied nose, bruise over his left eye — ole Ralph must have put up a real fight. I arrested him on the spot, read him his rights, and locked him up. Case solved.

Damis: Great job, Joe. I always knew you had instincts for detective work except ...

Joe: *(interrupts)* The police chief said I'll get a meritorious citation and a promotion. *(brags)* It's all in the eye — Damis — being perceptive and observant. And I have figured out why you've been feeling queasy each morning and it's so very silly of you — just because, Damis, we are going to get that dalmation puppy is no reason to get butterflies in your stomach. *(exits)*

Damis: Puppy? *(holds up an article of baby clothes — Joe doesn't see it)*

Joe: *(from offstage)* Yeah, just a dog — relax. We'll see you later, love.

Damis: *(incredulously as she looks at her large abdomen)* I'm having a puppy?

(Music plays as the lights fade.)

The End

Christmas Eve/Christmas Day
Cycle A

Looking For The Child Of Bethlehem

Texts: Isaiah 62:6-12; Psalm 97; Titus 3:4-7; Luke 2:(1-7) 8-20

Theme: Searching for the newborn babe

Characters:
    Leader
    Asher
    Innkeeper (nonspeaking)
    Innkeeper's Wife (nonspeaking)
    Innkeeper's Child (nonspeaking)
    Joseph (nonspeaking)
    Mary (nonspeaking)
    Shepherds (two or three, nonspeaking)
    Shopper 1
    Shopper 2
    Carolers (six to eight)
    Child
    Reader 1
    Reader 2

Tone: Devotional, thoughtful, joyful ending

Setting/Props:
    Appropriate biblical costumes
    Simple stable scene
    Papers
    Shopping bags for Shoppers
    Stools

Approximate time: 15-30 minutes

Production notes: Asher may use a hand microphone so he is free to move and can hold the microphone for other speakers. The Leader and Readers can speak from a lectern. Biblical costumes are needed for Asher, Joseph, Mary, the Shepherds, the Innkeeper, Innkeeper's Wife, and Innkeeper's Child.

Leader: We begin our worship, "Looking For The Child Of Bethlehem," by singing "O Come, O Come, Emmanuel," stanzas 1, 2, and 5.

(Asher enters from the rear at the start of Stanza 5, walks hesitantly through the audience, and moves to center stage. He looks around, confused. When the singing ends, he speaks.)

Asher: Excuse me. Am I interrupting something? I did hear the words, "Israel," "Emmanuel," and "Son of God," didn't I? Or am I hearing things? Perhaps I should leave. *(starts to leave, then stops)* No, I won't go! I must know what happened to him. Is what we heard true? Did he make a difference?

Leader: Excuse me, sir. May I help you?

Asher: I hope so. I've had very little help so far. I'm so confused. *(looks around)* Is this a church? I was told to find a church.

Leader: *(chuckles)* Of course, this is a church. This is ____(your)____ Church in ____(your town)____. Are you looking for someone in particular? I'm sure our pastor would talk to you.

Asher: I'm looking for a baby. But he wouldn't be a baby now. It all happened so long ago.

Leader: I think you should speak with our pastor.

Asher: I must find out about the baby. I have all my notes and questions on these papers. *(waves papers in the air)* I must learn what happened to that baby!

Leader: All right. Please calm down. I'm going to send someone to find our pastor right now.

Asher: *(shouting)* No! No! No leaders! The people must tell me — not their leaders. *(turns away)*

Leader: All right. It's just you and me and all these nice people here. *(motions to audience)* We're here to help you, if we can. Maybe it would help if you'd tell us a bit about yourself. Who are you? Where are you from?

Asher: *(still turned away)* Who am I? I am Asher, son of Omar. Where am I from? Now *that* is an interesting question. It might be more to the point to ask *when* I am from.

Leader: All right. *Where* are you from and *when* are you from?

Asher: My name is Asher. I was born in Bethlehem. Bethlehem is in Judea and is known as the city of David. I will tell you my story.

(Leader sits down.)

Asher: I am the son of an innkeeper in that faraway Bethlehem of which we spoke. How I came to be here, in this time and place, is something I can't explain. I am here. My story begins in Bethlehem nearly 2,000 years ago. There was a census ordered by the Romans, who occupied our land. They wanted to keep track of our numbers. Therefore, every Jew had to return to the place of his ancestor's birth to be registered and counted.

(Innkeeper, Innkeeper's Wife, and Innkeeper's Child enter from the side. Mary and Joseph enter at the rear and start down the center aisle at the same time. All proceed to the right side of the stage or chancel.)

Asher: Those were wonderful days for innkeepers. No vacancies every night. It was great! Soon we began to turn people away. Then one evening, a man and a very pregnant young woman arrived at our inn. Right from my first sight of them, I sensed they were different from the other travelers. We couldn't send them away. "The stable," I cried, "we could put them in the stable. They could rest there with the animals."

(Innkeeper's Child leads Mary and Joseph to left side of stage. Then the Innkeeper's family leaves by the side door. Mary sits on a low stool, and Joseph kneels by her side. Joseph hands her the baby.)

Asher: So I led Joseph and Mary to the stable, where she later gave birth to a baby. They named him "Jesus."

(Shepherds enter from side and flank Mary and Joseph.)

Asher: Now listen carefully to this, because this is the strange part. Shepherds from the fields surrounding Bethlehem came seeking the child. They said an angel had appeared to them and told them that their Savior was born in Bethlehem. Imagine! There we were claiming that the baby in a manger in our stable was the Messiah!

(Shepherds exit.)

Asher: The young family stayed in Bethlehem for a while after the census and then they fled from the city one dark night.

(Mary and Joseph exit hastily.)

Asher: Some say it was because of fear of King Herod and his terrible edict against male babies. As far as I know, they never returned to Bethlehem. Ever since that time, I've had questions. Was that baby Jesus really the Messiah? Many years later, stories were told of a teacher named Jesus who performed miracles. Later there came an incredible tale about him dying and rising from the dead. Could it be the same Jesus? *(pauses)*

(Leader returns to lectern.)

Asher: That is my story. I am still asking that question. Is the Jesus you speak of in your Christmas holiday the same Jesus I seek? Was the baby born in our stable really the Messiah? Did his birth and life change the world?

Leader: Wow! Now I can understand why you are so tired. Do you mean to say you've actually been going around asking people those questions? How did people react?

Asher: Yes, that is what I have done. At first I tried asking people on the street, but I soon found that they were only interested in hurrying back to their cars. Then I discovered your marketplace. I think you call it a mall. I found hundreds of people but many would not speak with me. Watch this typical encounter.

(Shoppers carrying shopping bags enter.)

Asher: *(approaches Shoppers)* Excuse me, please, I wonder if you could answer some questions for me.

Shopper 1: *(hesitantly)* Well, okay. But I don't have time for any kind of survey.

Asher: Thank you. Was the baby really the Messiah, and did his birth make a difference to the world?

Shopper 1: I'm sorry. I just don't have time for this.

Shopper 2: They really ought to screen you survey people more carefully. And look at that outfit! What next?

(Shoppers exit.)

Asher: My next encounter was with a singing group. I heard them referred to as carolers.

(Carolers enter singing "We Wish You A Merry Christmas.")

Asher: Excuse me. I enjoyed your song very much. Tell me, is it a Christmas song?

Caroler 1: Of course.

Caroler 2: What else?

Asher: Fine, fine, now tell me this: Could I learn about Jesus from this song?

Caroler 1: I guess not. But it is a Christmas song.

Caroler 2: Right. We didn't say it was a song about Jesus. It's a Christmas song.

Asher: Now maybe you can understand why I am confused. I continued to speak to people at the mall, asking each of them what Christmas means. I spoke to children, to women, to men. I heard about presents, parties, vacations from school, ski trips, cookies, family dinners. I was about to give up when I saw a line of children waiting to talk to an old gentlemen in a bright red suit. "Perhaps a child will have my answer," I thought. After all, it was a child who sent me on this quest.

(Child enters.)

Asher: *(to Child)* Hello, little one. Please don't be afraid of me. I want to ask you a question. Tell me, what is so special about this Christmas holiday?

Child: It's Jesus' birthday!

Asher: *(excitedly)* Did you say birthday? Did you say Jesus' birthday?

Child: Sure. Everyone knows that Christmas is Jesus' birthday.

Asher: Well, maybe not *everyone*. *(pauses)* Tell me, where can I learn more about this Jesus?

Child: Besides my mom and dad, I learn about Jesus in Sunday school and church. Maybe that's where you should go. *(exits)*

Asher: *(faces audience)* And that is how I happen to be here tonight. Is the Jesus of our stable honored in this church? Does his name have special meaning here? Have I come to the right place?

Leader: Asher, I could answer your questions with words. But I think the best idea would be for you to experience what we do in our church, as we, too, look for the child of Bethlehem. Sit down and join us as we hear God's word and sing praises to him.

Asher: Thank you.

(Asher sits on a stool facing the audience. Leader also sits down, and Reader 1 goes to the lectern. The Readers, in turn announce a scripture reading, read it, announce a hymn, and return to their seats.)

Reader 1: The first reading is Isaiah 40:1-5 and Isaiah 9:6-7. *(reads this text)* We will now sing "Come, Thou Long-Expected Jesus."

Reader 2: The second reading is Luke 2:1-20. *(read this gospel)* We will now sing "Hark! The Herald Angels Sing."

(Leader returns to the lectern and addresses Asher.)

Leader: Well, Asher, have we answered your questions?

Asher: Yes! Yes you have! My quest is over. My questions are answered at long last. I don't understand everything, but I can rest now. The prophecies, which I knew so well, have been fulfilled. "For unto us a Child is born, unto us a Son is given." I learned those words as a child. They are written on my heart. The child I have been seeking, the baby Jesus born in our stable in Bethlehem, is the same Jesus you honor in this church and continue to serve. He *is* the Messiah, come to set his people free. Praise the Lord!

Asher, Leader, and Readers: Thanks be to God!

Leader: *(to audience)* Let's stand and sing.

(Sing a Happy Christmas carol.)

The End

This sketch was written by Jean Ann Hillegass. It is reprinted with minor adaptations by permission of the author.

Christmas 1
Cycle A

Where's Dad?

Texts: Isaiah 63:7-9; Psalm 148; Hebrews 2:10-18; Matthew 2:13-23

Theme: Parenting, fathering (A preaching subject may be on Joseph as a fatherly role model.)

Characters:
　Brad Nelson
　Bowling Alley Proprietor
　Stranger

Tone: Thoughtful, emotionally painful

Setting/Props:
　Bowling alley setting with bowling balls
　Table and chairs
　Soda
　Telephone

Approximate time: 5-7 minutes

(Brad Nelson is sitting at a table sipping a soda. Bowling alley noises are heard in the background along with recorded Christmas carols. Bowling Alley Proprietor approaches Brad.)

Proprietor: Can I get you something,, sir? Did you want to bowl? We have an alley open now.

Brad: Naah, I'm really just waiting for someone — either I'm early or *he's* late — again!

Proprietor: Give me the high sign if you want something, buddy. *(exits)*

Brad: *(impatiently)* Okay, yeah, yeah. *(politely)* Thank you.

(Brad gets up and paces, while rehearsing what he's going to say and do.)

Brad: *(clears throat) Hello*, Dad. Hello, *Dad!* *(changes voices)* Hi, sir. *(tries again)* Hi, sir, er Dad. Happy Holiday. Merry Christmas! Long time no see. Naw. *(shakes head, sits down, twiddles nervously)*

Proprietor: *(offstage)* Paging Brad Nelson. Paging Brad Nelson. Line 2.

(Brad looks startled. He gets up quickly and looks for and finds a telephone.)

Brad: Hello, hello, this is Brad Nelson — Dad? Yeah, I'm here at Pitts Bowling Alley like we planned. Yes, I'm fine. What? You can't make it? *(pauses for imaginary conversation on the other end)* Well, what about what we had agreed to talk about? Yes, yes I know. But, but, Dad, I thought what we were going to talk about was pretty important, too. Dad, I'm 21 years old. I'm leaving tomorrow for Central America. I'll be gone at least a year — can't you just for once ... Oh, all right. *(dejectedly)* Yes, thank you, I'll have a safe trip. I'll let you know when I arrive. Bye. *(hangs up telephone, walks wearily to table)*

(Stranger is sitting at the table when Brad returns.)

Brad: Wha, what — excuse me this is *my* table and my drink. I was expecting someone!

Stranger: Oh, I'm sorry, I'll move, no problem.

Brad: *(embarrassed by own behavior)* No, no, that's okay. Sit. Sit. There's plenty of room. *(pauses)* You here to bowl?

Stranger: Hadn't planned to — actually, I'm just passing through town. A bowling alley right on the highway is pretty handy. I thought I'd drop in and get a cup of coffee. I'm actually headed for Centerville. I live there. Just celebrated Christmas with my brother and family in Nashville.

Brad: I see. *(extends hand)* I'm Brad Nelson. I was supposed to meet my dad but he just called — said his boss wanted him to check some blueprints and specs before bids tomorrow. It's deadline time for the project — but — that's the way it *always* is.

Stranger: You sound more than disappointed. Something wrong?

Brad: *(loudly blurts out)* Wouldn't you be if — *(speaks normally)* sorry, I don't even know you and here I am dumping my crap on you — I didn't mean to blow up!

Stranger: That's okay, son. I've got a boy about your age. I know he needs to vent now and then. Too much pent up stuff builds and builds until — boom — it's out!

Brad: Well, it ain't "now and then" it's more like now and now and now. You see, my dad is married to his work. I suppose he's a workaholic. We barely celebrated Christmas together. While the rest of us sang "Silent Night," Dad was singing and talking on his cellular phone at the same time. Can you believe he's been to *one* baseball game in the six years I was playing? Never made it to the school play I was in. True, Mom was sick much of the time, but one band concert, *I* was the trumpet soloist! *(angrily hits table)*

Stranger: Sure you're not just feeling sorry for yourself?

Brad: I am — I know — but I have felt so left out of his life. He played ball in the semi-pros and I tried to do the same, but never made it to first base — literally. *(stifles laugh)*

Stranger: Say, would you like to bowl a line?

Brad: Sure, why not?

(Brad and Stranger get up, check balls, and begin to bowl, making small talk about the game.)

Brad: Dad and I planned to talk today. Really talk. I have some unresolved issues to deal with. Since Mom died, Dad seems more mellow and open so we set up this "phantom" meeting. You see, sir, I'm leaving tomorrow for a year in Central America. I have too much emotional garbage to carry on that plane and all around the jungles. It's stressing me out.

Stranger: Like what?

Brad: Like when Mom was sick. I was going through tough times. Mom needed him but I needed him, too. "Dad, just play catch with me," I begged time and time again. "Show me how to throw a fastball." "Tomorrow," he always said. Well, tomorrow is still tomorrow. How would you feel if all of your life you were put off?

Stranger: Any brothers or sisters?

Brad: Yeah, there's Midge, my younger sister. And *that's* another deal.

Stranger: What do you mean, deal?

Brad: Midge this, Midge that. *(sarcastically)* The queen of the Nelson mansion. I understand the psychological father-daughter stuff but I not only played second fiddle to Midge, I played tenth fiddle. Call it sibling rivalry — call it what you will — Dad's apparent favoritism just leaked out all over, and I was always slipping and falling in it. All this anger I've got is not good. It's corroding my insides.

Stranger: So what were you going to say to your father? Were you going to tell him off?

Brad: Nope, I'm past that. We've had a couple of blowups and he got the message and did make some changes. But right now it's strictly adult to adult.

Stranger: So what *were* you going to say?

Brad: I *was* going to say the very things I had rehearsed.

Stranger: Rehearsed?

Brad: Yeah, like — Hi, Dad *(looks off into space)*, I know you love me, but so often I feel like I've been abandoned. I feel lonely, forgotten. Dad, I do love you and I know it's hard if not impossible for you to say back, "I love you, son." But try it! You'll like it! I think. And Dad, if you can't say, "I love you," just make up some phrase that means I love you like "Neener, Neener, num num."

Stranger: Neener, neener, num, num? *(laughs)*

Brad: I know it's dumb, kinda weird, but maybe it's a start to say, "Brad, neener, neener, num num." Then maybe ...

Stranger: I think it's easier to simply say, "I love you."

Brad: *(excitedly)* That's just the point! I don't think Dad could affirm me even if I won the lottery. Case in point: In 1994, I won the state sailing regatta title. I was elated. And my friends were dumbfounded. A guy ran up and kissed me on both cheeks. "I love you," he said. And I said, "Who are you?" He shouted, "I'm the guy who bet five bucks on you in the race and you made me win $5,000. Wow!" The next day the papers reported, "Norval Nelson's Son Wins The Annual Sailing Regatta." I felt I'd done something significant. Dad didn't say a word. Not even, "Nice job, son." Nothing. I know Dad's engineering work, Mom's sickness, and Midge's college pressures were on his mind but ... I've got an ache inside as big as a Mack truck. *(points to heart and wipes tear from his eye)*

Stranger: I see you desperately wanted to be noticed and loved. Like all of us, you want to be cared for and cared about. It's natural for any child. Adults, too. *I* still want attention and affirmation, and I'm 53. Your turn. Let's see you get a strike.

Brad: *(bowls)* Gutter ball! Typical! My luck.

Stranger: Well, take a deep breath and concentrate. Try again. Focus on succeeding.

(Brad bowls again and hits strike.)

Stranger: Great job!

Brad: Hey, maybe my luck's changing! Let's see how we've done thus far.

(They sit down and add up score.)

Stranger: Oops, there's my bus. I won't be able to finish the game, gotta be going. By the way my name's Stretch, George Stretch. Pleased to meet you. I hope things will go better for you and for your dad. In fact, I have a feeling after that last strike, Christmas ain't over yet. So long. *(waves and exits)*

Brad: Thanks for listening, Mr. Stretch — er — George. I feel a lot better, thanks to you. Bye now. *(pauses)*

Stranger: *(comes running back in)* Hey, Brad, there's a guy out in the parking lot getting his bowling ball out of the trunk of a Lincoln Continental. License plate has the name "Nelson" on it! Any relationship? Thought you'd like to know. Gotta go!

Brad: *(leaps up)* Yeess! *(high fives the startled Proprietor as he exits)*

The End

Christmas 2
Cycle A

The Difference Between Getting And Giving

Texts: Jeremiah 31:7-14; Psalm 147:13-21; Ephesians 1:3-14; John 1:(1-9) 10-18

Theme: Exploring the difference between selfish getting and gracious giving

Characters:
  Narrator
  Old Man
  Old Man's Pastor
  Former Girlfriend
  Beggar
  Man In Santa Claus Suit
  Devout Gentleman
  The Lord (or voice)

Tone: Humorous and thought-provoking

Setting/Props:
  Park bench
  Two chairs
  Bible
  Logo or sign suggesting "Heaven"
  Spotlight (to represent the Lord)
  Special white robe

Approximate time: 5-9 minutes

(The scene opens in a park. The Old Man is sitting on a bench pondering something deep.)

Narrator: Once there was an old man who didn't know the difference between giving and getting. It was sadly true — he had lived his whole life totally confused.
  His parents felt that children should be free to make up their own minds when they got old enough to think about those parts of life that are perfectly obvious. This completely confused him, and because of this confusion the old man had, on many occasions, been embarrassed about his lack of understanding.
  As the years passed, he finally stopped giving or receiving anything to avoid being ashamed in public. He had withdrawn into a sort of private loneliness that only a truly confused person can understand.
  At last, resolving to find out once and for all what giving and getting were all about, the old man set out on a long journey to consult those who had wisdom.

(Old Man gets up and moonwalks like Michael Jackson or makes walking motions or walks on a treadmill to simulate traveling.)

Narrator: First he went to the pastor of his former church where mix-ups during the offering had created enormous problems.

(Pastor appears, shakes hands with Old Man and they sit down.)

Narrator: Clearly distressed, the old man asked for a simple explanation.

Pastor: Brother, this business of giving and getting has obviously perplexed you a great deal and I can sympathize with you. But it's not that complicated, it's really very simple.

Old Man: Tell me, Pastor, tell me.

Pastor: It is more blessed to give than to receive! Furthermore, no one gives God anything. God has given us freely of God's bounteous store. We give back only what was God's in the first place. Therefore ...

Narrator: But that was enough of a simple explanation for the old man. He quietly and quickly slipped away while the pastor was expounding.

(Old Man gets up and tiptoes away.)

Narrator: Next, the old man visited a lovely woman who had taken a romantic interest in him.

(Former Girlfriend, extravagantly made-up, appears.)

Narrator: The romance had cooled when the old man kept *taking* presents instead of bringing them.

Former Girlfriend: I'll tell you the difference. When you give, you feel good, and when you receive, you feel better.

Narrator: The old man looked puzzled for a moment then asked:

Old Man: How are you supposed to know which is "good" and which is "better"?

Former Girlfriend: *(crossly)* What a silly question for an old man. I'm going to go to my apartment and write Christmas cards. I'm writing to all the people I forgot last year but who sent me a card anyway. That way I'll keep my *getting* even with my *giving*. *(exits)*

Narrator: Down the street, the old man met a beggar and wondered if this beggar person knew the difference between giving and getting.

Beggar: I'll teach you the difference between getting and giving my friend. Just give me your wallet. Hee hee.

Narrator: The old man was taken aback by the eagerness of this new would-be tutor.

Old Man: No, no, I'll figure this out with someone else. Thank you anyway for your kind offer.

Beggar: Oh, the munificence and beneficence and pecuniary philanthropies of the human species. *(walks off)*

Narrator: Shortly after this brief encounter with the beggar man, the old man chanced upon a nattily attired personage.

(Man In Santa Claus Suit appears, busily working the crowd.)

Old Man: Certainly this man in the fur-lined red suit must know the fine points of the giving and getting dichotomy. Hey you.

Man In Santa Claus Suit: Who me?

Old Man: Yeah, you.

Man In Santa Claus Suit: What do you want?

Old Man: You seem to be a generous personage. Can you enlighten me on the difference between getting and giving? I know it's a philosophical question that has its practical applications but I'm really confused.

Man In Santa Claus Suit: How should I know? I just do this routine for a job! Ask somebody who isn't busy listening to other people's kids nag and whine all day like I have to put up with. This is a real pain. Oh my aching back, my sore feet. *(cranks up his voice to the proper pitch and tone)* Ho, ho, ho! *(continues to fake being jolly)* Happy holiday, everybody! Ho, ho, ho!

Narrator: The old man plodded on wondering what it all meant.

(Old Man walks on.)

Narrator: His next stop was at the home of a devout gentleman who was at the very moment reading a properly threadbare leather-bound copy of the Bible. It took only one deft flick of the wrist to find the correct passage to explain how giving and getting differed.

Devout Gentleman: See here, my good fellow. In the gospel of our Lord according to Saint Luke, in chapter 6, verses 30 through 31 and verse 38, we read thusly....

Narrator: The gentleman was obviously schooled in Bible and theology and he read quite a puzzling array of verses about giving to everyone who asks, and doing to other people the things you want to get back from them, and God giving to you when you've given to others.

Devout Gentleman: And furthermore ...

Old Man: *(interrupts, stressed)* But I don't see how giving and getting are all that different if every time you give you get back, and if everything you get you're supposed to give away.

Devout Gentleman: If my answers are not adequate, you've got a problem! You'll have to ask God this question that seems to be burning its way into your very soul. Perhaps God has the solution.

(Old Man sits down on bench, then lies down on it.)

Narrator: Well, that's exactly what happened. After weeks of going to people who seemed to know the difference but still couldn't explain it satisfactorily, the old man died quietly in his sleep, troubled but hopeful that God would at last answer his questions. And by golly, God certainly did.

(Old Man gets up, now wearing a special white robe to denote a transformation.)

Narrator: Upon his entrance into heaven, the old man was met by the Lord, who took just a few short minutes to clear up the entire matter.

(Lord appears in the form of a light.)

Narrator: With a smile of complete understanding, the old man took his place with the rest of the saints and gave God praise for all the blessings he had received. And that's the story of the old man ... What did God tell him? Well, the difference between giving and getting is so simple that everyone *knows* what God said! Well, doesn't everyone...?

The End

Adapted from the *Alternatives* newsletter article, "Giving Means Getting Means Giving: A Parable for Advent." Used by permission. © *Alternatives*, Box 2857, Sioux City, Iowa 51106.

Bonus Advent Sketch
Cycle A

Prepare: An Advent Play

Texts: General Advent

Theme: Prepare for Christmas in the proper way. Advent is for repentance and change.

Characters:
    Santa Claus (dressed in traditional Santa suit with beard and hat)
    John The Baptist (dressed in rough burlap material and sandals)

Tone: Humorous, serious, provoking

Setting/Props:
    Large Santa bag
    Wrapped presents
    Toys for Santa's bag
    List
    The setting can be anywhere

Approximate time: 7-8 minutes

(John the Baptist enters singing "Prepare Ye" from Godspell *or a favorite Advent hymn verse.)*

John: *(shouts)* People of God! I am John the Baptist, son of Zachariah and Elizabeth. I've just come from the desert. *(shakes off dust)* And I have a message of great importance for you. *(points to the audience)* It's this: It's time to wake up! Get ready! Change your ways — the Advent of our Lord King is near. (*) I see you are already preparing for something. What the?

*(*At this point, Santa, carrying his bag full of toys, appears singing "Jolly Old St. Nicholas" or "Here Comes Santa Claus.")*

Santa: Hi from the North Pole, folks. My name is Santa Claus. I've dropped by to help John B. here and all of you to prepare for Christmas.

John: You're going to what? Help *me*, oh fat one? Since when?

Santa: *(jolly)* You bet! I heard that you and these people here *(to congregation)* are preparing for Christmas and since Christmas is my business, here I am. *(roars with laughter)* (Name of keyboardist), let's get everybody in the Christmas spirit by singing a Christmas carol or two. How about "Jingle Bells"? *(motions for everyone to sing)* "Dashing through the snow...." *(begins to hand out the toys and gifts in his bag)*

John: Wait a minute! Hold everything, Mr. Fat, Jolly One! What in blazes do you think you're doing? This is not the preparation I came to announce. *(sings "Prepare ye the way of the Lord, Prepare ye ...")*

Santa: *(interrupts)* Of course, John B., how else can these folks get ready. *(hums "Jingle Bells")* There are only (number) shopping days left, folks. Here's the *TV Guide*. TV shopping is on channel (number). *(brightly)* And the malls are open 'til 10 o'clock every night. Wow! Can you believe it? Such convenience. *(shouts)* Bring your little ones, I'll be there — lap and all — I'll promise 'em whatever they desire.

John: Stop it, Mr. Claus.

Santa: Just call me Santa Claus.

John: Santa Claus, Santa humbug. You're out to lunch. I came to tell these folks here, to prepare for the coming....

Santa: *(interrupts)* Cool it, John B. Take it easy. Everybody knows that the way you prepare is by buying things. Here I have some sample Christmas cards, a list of places to get your tree, and then go to Santa's wonderland at the shops at the mall, Christmas baskets at the Salvation Army, and here, look at the instructions for mailing packages from the post office.

John: Hold it! Hold everything! There's a big omission here. You haven't even mentioned the prophecies of the Old Testament. Have you forgotten the promise of the Messiah, the Savior, who would come and save the world? The season of Advent is a time to repent, not repaint. A time to reflect, not replenish your things. I am here to help you prepare in the right way. And for all your extravagance and waste and sin, don't you feel any regret or grief or sorrow? Any guilt? Any contrition?

Santa: Ho, ho, ho! This is the season of jolliness, John B. Who wants reflection and contemplation and all that? It's party time! Strike up the band. *(starts to sing "Rudolph, The Red-Nosed Reindeer," invites audience to join in, and hands out trinkets)*

John: *(waves hands to stop)* Oh, I know it's fun to sing those songs at Christmas but its ADVENT! AD—VENT! *(sings a verse of "Prepare The Royal Highway")*

Santa: *(describes some new Christmas items that are current bestsellers while John is singing)* Well, I see my bag is almost empty. I wonder if I'm missing anything.

John: This is ridiculous! You ought to know better, Santa. Why your origin and roots go back to Saint Nicholas that kindly, generous bishop of Myra. He was a Christian. You don't prepare for Christmas simply by seeing how many gifts you can buy or lights you can put up on your house or place of business. It's the light in your heart from God's Word that makes the difference. Your gifts are fine, Santa, but the important gift is God's Son born in a manger and who eventually died on the cross for your sins and mine. I know a Christmas song that can tame the most extravagant impulses. *(sings a verse of "O Little Town Of Bethlehem")*

Santa: *(quiet and thoughtful)* Oh? Mmm. *(pauses, strokes beard, then slowly takes off hat in reverence)* John B., I believe I'm beginning to catch on. There's more to this celebration than what we're getting ready for in my workshop at the North Pole with all my elves, my reindeer, and sleigh — I know that I am really mythical and fanciful ... you know ... mmm ... and what you speak of rings true — amazing but true ... God coming to earth in Jesus. Oh, my! Oh, my goodness!

John: That's right, Santa. Now you're getting it. I love your spirit and enthusiasm, though, Santa. Giving and generosity is exactly like the generosity of God's love. Gifts to the poor and unfortunate are right on. And we don't give because boys and girls are good or bad. We give out of pure thankfulness and gratitude for God's wonderful grace in the babe.

Santa: So you're not going to try to get rid of me?

John: No, no, Santa, just trying to redirect you and your efforts. We've got to get ready — the celebration of Christ's birth is just __(number)__ days away.

Santa: I know   don't I know.

John: When I say, "Repent, for the kingdom of heaven is here, Prepare the way of the Lord, make his paths straight," and then I baptize people for the repentance of sin — you know Santa, they experience an exciting joy and freedom they've never had before. You can just see it in their faces. And it shows in their lives. Do you want to be baptized Santa?

Santa: Uh, er — I believe I was baptized — at least my historical character Saint Nicholas was. Is that valid?

John: Oh yes — as long as you believe and trust God's promises. Repent daily and follow Christ with all your heart. *(exits singing "O Come, O Come, Emmanuel" or "Baptized" by Jay Beech)*

Santa: *(reflective)* What a revelation. Am I glad I met John B. Now I know God loves me and will keep after me even when I get overwhelmed with worldly things. I thought *more* was better, but in one sense *less* is better. I thought Christmas decorating was the beauty of Christmas but it's the decoration in the *heart*, not the *hearth*, that is important. I love holly and I want to be jolly — but for a different reason — thanks to John B. *(exits singing, "Prepare Ye")*

The End

Adapted by Arley Fadness and reprinted with permission of *Modern Liturgy*, © copyright 1978, Vol. 5, No. 7, 60 East Virginia Street #290, San Jose, California 95112.

Synopses Of The Mini-Dramas For Cycle B

The Ball Game
Two men at a ball game discuss their day. One is frustrated with all the waiting he had to do. The two discuss the pros and cons of waiting. They discover a good side to waiting. The sketch is an excellent set up for preaching the importance of "waiting" for God's redemption.

The Waiting Man
A man standing by a shopping mall door is waiting for someone really special to come along. Various people inquire about who it is he is waiting for. The curious questioners build for an answer to be addressed later in the sermon.

The Waiting Room
Several people wait in a doctor's waiting room to see the doctor. Each has a malady. One waiting person, however, does not know what is wrong with his wife. In the end, the nurse announces to his surprise, that he will be a father.

For What Do We Wait?
Another scene in the doctor's waiting room where several people express what they are waiting for in life. One person is waiting for something really exciting. It turns out to be a baby that he learns his wife has just delivered.

Stable Talk
The scene is in the stable near the manger. Mary is half-lying on a couch-like bench while Joseph is standing or sitting as is appropriate. (Two people in a donkey suit could add a little comic relief by standing nearby taking in every word. This would have to be done delicately so as not to detract from the dialogue.)

Two Futures
A child speaks while playing with a yo-yo or similar toy, and wonders out loud about his or her future. Then two people, men or women, representing a specific parental style begin to speak alternately. They stand together with bodies turned away from each other about thirty degrees. The child may sit down in the front or play quietly in the background. The dialogue contrasts two opposing ways of rearing, disciplining, and nurturing a child.

The Adoption
Two siblings overhear their parents make plans to use the extra room in their home for a family addition. They siblings misunderstand the parents' intentions. The parents intend to adopt a child from China, but the children think they are getting an exotic pet from the zoo or an abandoned animal from the humane society.

**Advent 1
Cycle B**

The Ball Game

Texts: Isaiah 64:1-9; Psalm 80:1-7, 17-19; 1 Corinthians 1:3-9; Mark 13:24-47

Theme: Some things are worth waiting for

Characters:
   Bill
   Frank

Tone: Frustration, impatience, anticipation

Setting/Props:
   Baseball caps
   Baseball glove
   Two glasses
   Row of chairs (to represent bleachers at a stadium)
   Baseball (thrown toward Bill and Frank to simulate a foul ball)

Approximate time: 5 minutes

(Bill and Frank enter the stadium anxious to watch the baseball game. They wear appropriate baseball caps. Frank has his glove and Bill carries two glasses of pop. Bill is visibly upset by having to wait in line to get in and buy the pop.)

Bill: Boy, Frank, I never thought we were gonna get in here! What a line!

Frank: Yeah, it was kind of long. But, hey, Bill, forget it. We've got front row seats, third-base side right behind the dugout! Here they are. *(sits down)*

Bill: Forget it? I can't forget it. It seems like I've been waiting for something or somebody all day! I'm fed up!

Frank: Oh, come on! Sit down, gimme my pop, and relax. This is gonna be great! *(pounds his glove)*

Bill: *(sits)* That's easy for you to say. You didn't have the kind of day I did.

Frank: *(excitedly)* Hey, here comes the wave!

(They do the wave.)

Frank: Sounds like your day didn't go too well. Want to tell me about it?

Bill: You're sure you want to hear it?

Frank: Sure, I do.

Bill: Well, it all started this morning at home. I was running behind getting ready for work and needed to get in the bathroom.

Frank: Don't tell me, lemme guess, your daughter was in there moussing her hair.

Bill: No, my *son* was! I had to wait for *him*!

Frank: Well, okay, so then what?

Bill: I left the house late and ran to the bus stop. I saw the bus turning the corner to leave just as I came around the corner. I had to *wait* about fifteen minutes for the next bus.

Frank: *(in mocked horror)* Oh — fifteen minutes! How awful! Go on.

Bill: By the time I got downtown I was hungry. I hadn't had time for breakfast, so I stopped at Mac and Don's for a quick bite. Wouldn't you know, they didn't have enough help on duty and I wasted ten minutes there.

Frank: *(excitedly)* Here it comes again.

(They do the wave again.)

Bill: I finally got to work and just missed the elevator. I waited in the lobby for five minutes — then decided I could just as well walk up, so I did ... all seventeen floors!

Frank: No wonder you're draggin'.

Bill: The real clincher came at work, though. By the time I got there, I was so late that my boss had hired somebody named Bob from Accountemps to fill in for me that day!

Frank: Noooo!

Bill: Yessss! My boss, George Begelowe, told me to take the rest of the day off. He said the stuff could wait!

(They do the wave again.)

Frank: Sounds like you've been running all day.

Bill: That's not the point. The point is, I've had to *wait* all day. *Wait* for my son, *wait* for the bus, *wait* for my food, *wait* for the elevator. And then — and then — I had to *wait* to get in there and *wait* to get served at the concession stand! I've *waited* enough today to last a year!

(pause)

Frank: You know, Bill, waiting isn't always such a bad thing.

Bill: Hurumph.

Frank: No, really.

Bill: What are you trying to do? Cheer me up?

Frank: I'm just saying that waiting has its good side, too.

Bill: That's a laugh.

Frank: No, I'm serious, waiting can be really good.

Bill: No way.

Frank: Sure it can. Look, there are some things we don't mind waiting for, aren't there? Take your garden. When you plant your seeds in the spring you don't plan to harvest them the next day. You wait until they're mature and then you enjoy them.

Bill: Yeah, that's different.

Frank: Or what about a couple who want to start a family? They just don't get instant kids ya-know. Whether you have them by adoption or naturally it all takes time, but it makes the actual event that much sweeter. Sometimes it takes patience.

Bill: I'm not convinced.

Frank: *(turns and yells at peanut vendor)* Hey, can we get some peanuts down here someday this week? *(turns to Bill)* Now where was I?

Bill: "Sometimes it takes patience."

Frank: Oh yeah, like I was saying, sometimes it takes patience.

(They do the wave again.)

Frank: What inning are we in?

Bill: The third. Can I use your glove for a few innings?

Frank: Sure, now see, that's my point.

Bill: What point?

Frank: About waiting and being patient. You wouldn't want the game to be over already would ya?

Bill: No, I paid my money. I want to see the whole thing.

Frank: That's right, and it wouldn't be a ball game if it wasn't the whole thing, say if they cut out the middle innings now would it? Being able to *wait* for something really is a gift.

Bill: A what?

Frank: A gift. I mean you can see *waiting* as an opportunity.

Bill: An opportunity for what?

Frank: An opportunity to enjoy something at its fullest for instance. Like this game. Or an opportunity to step back and take stock in yourself or your situation. See where you are, where you've been and where you're goin! It gives us a chance to clear the air and establish a direction again. We need to do that from time to time. That's what *waiting* can do for ya.

Bill: Hey, Frank, look out! There's a foul coming our way!

(A ball is lobbed from the congregation, and Bill catches it with a bit of theatrics.)

Bill: Wow, I got it! I've never caught a foul ball here in my life!

Frank: Bill, that's great! Good thing you had my glove! Well, maybe this day is going to end better than it began.

Bill: Yeah, I guess it was worth the *wait*!

The End

Written by Jay Beech and Dave Eliason.

Advent 2
Cycle B

The Waiting Man

Texts: Isaiah 40:1-11; Psalm 85:1-2, 8-13; 2 Peter 3:8-15a; Mark 1:1-8

Theme: Waiting for someone — really special

Characters:
    Passerby
    Waiting Man
    Spouse
    Person 1
    Person 2
    Teen 1
    Teen 2

Tone: Mysterious

Setting/Props:
    Mall door backdrop (optional)
    Shopping bags
    Books
    Rollerblades

Approximate time: 5 minutes

(A man is waiting by a door in a shopping mall. He appears bored and is shuffling his feet and whistling. He is approached by another person. They do not know one another.)

Passerby: *(causally)* What's happening?

Waiting Man: I'm just waiting.

Passerby: Oh, yeah? Man, don't you hate to wait?

Waiting Man: Yeah. I guess everybody does. *(pauses)*

Passerby: What are you waiting for?

Waiting Man: I'm not at liberty to say.

Passerby: Oh, sorry. Didn't mean to pry. *(pauses)* Been waiting long?

Waiting Man: Yes, quite a while now.

Passerby: Must be something pretty important, that you're waiting for, I mean.

Waiting Man: It's really important. Of critical importance, you could say.

Passerby: But you can't discuss it.

Waiting Man: Please.

Passerby: Sorry, sorry, I'm just curious. Naturally curious, I guess.

(Waiting Man turns his attention back to the door. Passerby is joined by Spouse who is carrying shopping bags.)

Spouse: Hi, honey.

Passerby: Hi. *(whispers)* There seems to be something kind of unusual going on here. This guy is waiting for something, and I think it's something pretty big. But he won't tell me what it is.

Spouse: Well, why should he tell you?

Passerby: That's what's so weird. He *told* me he's waiting for something really important. He kind of teased me, sort of baited me, and then left me hanging.

Spouse: Huh. He is kind of smug looking, isn't he?

Passerby: Very suspicious, if you ask me.

Spouse: Like he's hiding something.

(Passerby and Spouse nod. Person 1 and Person 2 approach carrying books.)

Person 1: *(excitedly)* Excuse me, is this the line for the Geraldo book signing?

Person 2: *(dramatically)* Now, it can be told.

(Person 1 and Person 2 laugh.)

Passerby: No, I don't think so.

Person 1: Well then, what are you waiting for?

Spouse: We're not waiting but this guy is. He's waiting for something really important.

Passerby: Yeah, and he won't tell us what it is.

Person 2: Maybe he won the lottery and doesn't want anyone to steal his ticket.

Person 1: Or maybe he's with the Secret Service and the president is down shopping at JC Penney's again.

Spouse: Or maybe he's a hit man or a drug dealer or something.

(All slowly turn their heads toward Waiting Man and look at him suspiciously.)

Passerby: Well, whatever he's waiting for, I'll tell you one thing, I'm not going to miss it.

(As all nod their heads in agreement, two teenagers rollerblade up to the group and get in line.)

Teen 1: What are we in line for?

Person 2: We have no idea.

(Teen 1 and Teen 2 look at one another — puzzled.)

Teen 1 and Teen 2: *(pause)* Cool!

(Attention turns to Waiting Man who is looking earnestly through the door and becoming excited as he apparently sees what he has been waiting for. All the others crowd around in anticipation.)

Passerby: Hey! I think this it is.

(All crowd behind Waiting Man even closer, murmuring excitedly and straining to see.)

Waiting Man: *(to unseen person)* I can't believe you're finally here. This is the greatest moment of my life! I would have waited forever! *(passes through the door to join his companion)*

(All are stunned.)

Person 1: That was it?

Spouse: I can't believe we wasted our time waiting around for that.

Teen 2: That was really exciting.

Teen 1 and Teen 2: *(look at each other)* Not!

Passerby: I will *never* understand what that was all about.

Person 2: Come on, let's get out of here. Oprah's coming on. We can watch it down at Kmart.

(All agree and exit together, talking to each other as music fades.)

The End

Written by Jay Beech and David Eliason.

**Advent 3
Cycle B**

The Waiting Room

Texts: Isaiah 61:1-4, 8-11; Psalm 126 or Luke 1:47-55; 1 Thessalonians 5:16-24; John 1:6-8, 19-28

Theme: Waiting for a baby

Characters:
    Mr. Rush
    Vickie
    Mrs. Hornblower
    Nurse
    Waiting Man
    Stagehand (nonspeaking)

Tone: Humorous, surprise ending

Setting/Props:
    Waiting room setting with chairs
    Sling
    Tissues
    Sign with "30 minutes lapse" printed on it
    List

Approximate time: 5 minutes

(The scene opens up in a doctor's waiting room. Waiting Man is visibly worried. Mr. Rush, his arm in a sling, paces impatiently. Vickie sits in a chair. She has the hiccups. Mrs. Hornblower enters with a bad cold. She has boxes of Kleenex with her and blows her nose occasionlly. She sits as the scene opens.)

Mr. Rush: Boy, I don't know what's taking so long. I've been waiting here nearly an hour.

Vickie: Whatcha here for, mister? *(hiccups)*

Mr. Rush: They're just gonna check my arm, make sure it's healing okay. It'll only take a minute ... if I ever get in there!

Mrs. Hornblower: Sir, why don't you just calm down. You're making me nervous. *(sneezes, blows nose)*

Mr. Rush: You're nervous, I'm the one who's nervous! I'm half an hour late for a very important meeting! *(gestures with arms, hurts self in the process)* Ow! Now, look what you made me do!

Vickie: *(to Mrs. Hornblower)* Awe, don't mind him. *(hiccups)* He's been like that the whole time he's been here. Got a bad cold, huh? *(hiccups)*

Mrs. Hornblower: I sure do. *(blows nose)* I haven't slept in a week. The store loves to see me coming. I've bought so many boxes of tissues there that they're gonna give me my own special.

Vickie: That's a lot of tissues. *(hiccups)*

Mrs. Hornblower: I just want some relief. I thought this would clear up by itself but it doesn't seem to want to go away. I've waited as long as I can. *(blows nose)*

(Nurse enters.)

Nurse: Mrs. Hornblower.

(Mrs. Hornblower stands and exits with Nurse.)

Mr. Rush: Hey, how'd she get in there so quick? She just got here! I've been waiting for an hour! *(keeps pacing, then approaches Vickie)* What's your problem?

Vickie: Can't you tell? *(hiccups)* I've got the hiccups! *(hiccups)*

Mr. Rush: Hiccups? That doesn't sound very serious.

Vickie: Well, I've had them for three days! *(hiccups)*

Mr. Rush: Ooooh, that is quite a while. Does it bother you?

Vickie: Not really, I don't even notice anymore *(hiccups)* but my teacher made me come to see the doctor.

Mr. Rush: Your teacher? Why?

Vickie: Well, my class was taking final tests yesterday and I hiccuped through the whole thing. *(hiccups)* We all did badly and my teacher thinks I wrecked the curve! *(hiccups)* I just hope I don't have to get a shot! *(hiccups)*

Mr. Rush: Now I've heard everything, but I suppose it ...

(Nurse enters, interrupting Mr. Rush.)

Nurse: Vickie.

(Vickie exits with Nurse.)

Mr. Rush: How do you like that? *(gestures with good arm again and hurts self)* Owww!

(Stagehand walks by with a sign that reads "30 minutes elapse.")

Mrs. Hornblower: *(re-enters, approaches Mr. Rush)* Still here?

Mr. Rush: Yes, no thanks to you.

Mrs. Hornblower: Relax, your time will come. *(exits)*

Mr. Rush: *(toward Waiting Man)* Well, I guess it's just the two of us. My name is Rush, what's yours?

Waiting Man: That's not important right now.

Mr. Rush: Say, you've been awfully quiet. What's wrong with you, are you really sick? *(sits down)*

Waiting Man: It's not me, it's my wife.

Mr. Rush: You look worried.

Waiting Man: I am very worried. She's been sick for several weeks and we don't know what's wrong with her. She's never sick. I just don't know what to do.

Mr. Rush: Now, I'm sure they'll be able to help her. There are good doctors here *(looks over his shoulder)* ... if they ever let you in!

Waiting Man: I'm not very good at waiting especially for the unknown. I just wish I knew what the problem was. That would make it easier. It's just this not knowing.

(Vickie and Nurse reappear, interrupting Waiting Man.)

Nurse: I hope that medicine cures your hiccups, Vickie, good-bye. *(looks at list)* Mr. Rush.

Mr. Rush: I don't believe it! I'm finally getting in! Call the newspaper, this should make the front page.

Nurse: Right this way, sir.

(Nurse and Mr. Rush exit.)

Vickie: *(toward Waiting Man)* Are you still here?

Waiting Man: I'm waiting for my wife.

Vickie: What's wrong with her?

Waiting Man: We don't know. That's why I'm worried.

Vickie: I saw some lady in there, maybe it was your wife.

Waiting Man: How was she? How'd she look? Is she okay?

Vickie: I couldn't tell, they closed the door. Don't worry, I'm sure she's in good hands and she'll be okay.

Waiting Man: I hope you're right. I can't take much more waiting.

(Mr. Rush and Nurse reenter. Mr. Rush has an additional sling on the other arm.)

Nurse: Be sure to come back and see us next week.

Mr. Rush: Maybe I should start waiting now, then I'd get in on time!

Waiting Man: *(stands)* Please, can you tell me how my wife is? I've been waiting so long, I'm very worried.

Nurse: Yes, I knew that you were both worried when you came in today. But I have some good news for you.

Waiting Man: What is it? Ulcer? Gall bladder?

Nurse: *(laughs)* No, you're going to be a father. Your wife is going to have a baby!

Waiting Man: A b-b-b-baby?

Vickie: Wow, neato!

Mr. Rush: I don't believe it!

Nurse: Would you like to see her?

Waiting Man: I certainly would!

(Nurse and Waiting Man exit.)

The End

Written by Jay Beech and David Eliason.

**Advent 4
Cycle B**

For What Do We Wait?

Texts: 2 Samuel 7:1-11, 16; Luke 1:47-55 or Psalm 89:1-4, 19-26; Romans 16:25-27; Luke 1:26-38

Theme: Waiting

Characters:
  Nurse
  Waiting Man
  Mrs. Abernathy
  Bart
  Suzie
  Mr. Schwartz
  Bonnie

Tone: Light, humorous

Setting/Props:
  Waiting room setting with chairs
  Scrubs
  Coffee cups
  Coat

Approximate time: 5 minutes

(The scene is in a hospital waiting room. Waiting Man, dressed in scrubs, is seated surrounded by cups of coffee. He is very nervous. Nurse is talking to him. Mrs. Abernathy, Suzie, and Bonnie are seated with him. Mr. Schwartz stands leaning against the wall.)

Nurse: Are you feeling all right now, sir?

Waiting Man: Yeah, I'm okay, but I feel kinda foolish.

Nurse: Don't worry. It's not uncommon for someone to faint in the delivery room.

Waiting Man: Maybe, but I wanted to be there for my wife.

Nurse: I know. But I think it's better if you just wait here now. I'll come and get you as soon as we know something.

Waiting Man: Thanks.

Nurse: Mrs. Abernathy.

Mrs. Abernathy: *(growls)* About time!

(Nurse and Mrs. Abernathy exit as Bart enters.)

Bart: Hi, Suzie.

Suzie: Hi, Bart.

Bart: How long have you been waiting? *(takes off coat and sits)*

Suzie: I just got here, but I think these other people have been waiting quite a while.

Bart: Boy, I hope I don't have to wait too long. I've got to get home before the letter carrier gets there. My grades are coming today and I've got to see 'em before Dad does!

Suzie: How come?

Bart: I've got to make sure my grades are high enough. If I don't stay eligible for basketball, my dad'll kill me! If I can just pass biology, everything'll be all right.

Suzie: You might be waiting for your grades but I'm waiting for something really important.

Bart: What's that?

Suzie: My allowance.

Bart: Your allowance?

Suzie: Yeah, then I can go to the mall. I need a pair of designer jeans.

Bart: Why?

Suzie: You know as well as I that if you don't have the right clothes, you just don't fit in. I'm not gonna let that happen! When you look good, life is cool.

Mr. Schwartz: I couldn't help but overhear your conversation about what you're waiting for. You know what I'm waiting for?

Suzie: No, what?

Mr. Schwartz: I'm waiting for the perfect job, the job that'll launch my career and put me on easy street. Then I'll be livin'!

Bart: What makes you think you're gonna find this perfect job?

Mr. Schwartz: Because I'm so sufficiently qualified! I just finished six years of post-secondary education at MIT. I've taken my GREs, I've got my MBA, and I'm working on a PHD. I drive an SUV, my dad works for IBM, I may hook up with the CIA or the FBI, and I wear BVD's!

Bonnie: *(perks up her ears and enters the conversation)* Oh my, you certainly are qualified for ... for something!

Mr. Schwartz: Yes, I certainly am. Perhaps best of all, I saved the best for last, I am a close personal friend of Arnold Schwarzenegger!

Bart: Noooooo! Schwartz and Schwarzenegger?

Mr. Schwartz: I am, and let me tell you, he can really open doors for a person.

Bonnie: Speaking of doors, I wonder when we're gonna get in to see the doctor?

Mr. Schwartz: Yeah, they are pretty slow today. Kind of reminds me of the army, hurry up and wait.

(Nurse enters with Mrs. Abernathy.)

Nurse: We'll see you next week, Mrs. Abernathy. Don't forget your prescription. Suzie.

(Suzie and Nurse exit.)

Mrs. Abernathy: I suppose this prescription will cost me a fortune. It's just me and my kids at home, you know. It's tough to make it on one income, and they're certainly no help. Lazy, that's what they are. Good for nothin! I can't wait until they're gone and outta my hair. Then I'll have some extra spending money and maybe some peace of mind. I just can't wait.

Bonnie: Well, as long as everybody is volunteering to share what they're waiting for, I might as well, too.

Mrs. Abernathy: This oughta be interesting.

Bonnie: I'm waiting for the perfect man, Mr. Right, someone who'll sweep me off my feet and with whom I'll live happily ever after.

Mrs. Abernathy: Honey, you're gonna be waitin' a long, long time! I don't know anybody like that. *(speaks as she exits)*

Bonnie: And I don't either, but it's only a matter of time. And I've got all the time in the world. I can wait!

Bart: Well, I'm getting sick of waiting. I have to beat that letter carrier home.

Mr. Schwartz: *(to Waiting Man)* How about you? What are you waiting for? We've all shared our stories. What's yours?

Bonnie: Are you waiting for something fun? Like maybe a vacation to Bermuda?

Bart: Yeah, you've been awfully quiet, mister. What are you waiting for, anyway?

Waiting Man: I'm waiting for something very exciting.

Bonnie: Oooohh, maybe you're going to get married.

Mr. Schwartz: Exciting, huh? Maybe you're a *Reader's Digest* Sweepstakes winner.

Bart: I bet somebody's got Super Bowl tickets for you and you're waiting to get 'em!

Waiting Man: I'm afraid you're not on the right track at all.

Bonnie: Well, what is the right track? You said it was exciting.

Mr. Schwartz: Yeah, what are you waiting for?

Waiting Man: I'm waiting for a ... a ... a baby!

Bart: A baby? That's the dumbest thing I ever heard! All they do is cry and keep you up all night.

Mr. Schwartz: Babies are certainly not a good investment. I've heard it costs over $120,000 to raise a kid today! Way too much money.

Bonnie: And they're so messy! I would never want one.

Mr. Schwartz: I think you'd better reprioritize what you're waiting for. Think again.

(Nurse enters with Suzie, then walks toward Waiting Man.)

Nurse: *(smiles)* I have some wonderful news for you. Your wife has just delivered a healthy baby girl. Would you like to see them?

Waiting Man: *(very happily)* A girl, we have a baby girl! Yes, I'd love to see them. I can't wait!

(Nurse and Waiting Man exit.)

Suzie: Wow, did you see how happy he was?

Bart: Yeah, he was floatin'!

Bonnie: Can a baby do that to you?

Mr. Schwartz: Well, I guess maybe it can.

The End

Written by Jay Beech and David Eliason.

**Christmas Eve/Christmas Day
Cycle B**

Stable Talk

Texts: Isaiah 9:2-7; Psalm 96; Titus 2:11-14; Luke 2:1-14 (15-20)

Theme: The loving couple discuss the amazing events

Characters:
  Mary
  Joseph
  Elizabeth
  Baby Jesus
  Nosey Donkey (optional)

Tone: Mellow, warm

Setting/Props:
  Stable setting with manger
  Bench
  Doll or actual baby

Note: Two people in a donkey suit could add a little comic relief by standing nearby taking in every word. This would have to be done delicately so as not to detract from the dialogue.

Approximate time: 5-6 minutes

Scene 1
(This scene takes place in the stable near the manger. Mary is half lying on the bench, while Joseph is sitting beside her.)

Joseph: How are you feeling now my beloved?

Mary: Much better. It just takes time and rest.

Joseph: I was worried.

Mary: I know.

Joseph: First delivery can be hard — and with no help.

Mary: It was kinda tough. But look, Joseph dear, at this beautiful baby the Lord has brought to us.

Joseph: Oh yes — let me hold him —

Mary: Careful!

Joseph: Yes, I will be careful — he's only hours old ... so ruddy ... you little prune ... *(makes doting father noises)*

Mary: I can hardly believe the incredible events that have happened these past weeks.

Joseph: Which specifically, Mary?

Mary: Well, when that "presence" came and I felt myself actually conversing with, with —

Joseph: With what Mary?

Mary: With — it seemed like — an ... an *angel*!

Joseph: An angel? You, too?

Mary: And why do you say, "You, too," Joseph, my love? Do you believe in angels?

Joseph: Well, I don't know, but I too, had a "presence" or overwhelming feeling speak to me in a dream when we were just engaged. But tell me your story first Mary.

Mary: *(strokes Joseph's face)* You are so gracious, Joseph. I do love you.

Joseph: And I love you, Mary.

Mary: Well, after the news came out that Elizabeth was pregnant ... I went to her ... you know how barren Elizabeth was — they had waited so long for a baby ...

(Joseph freezes and Mary moves to another scene site.)

Scene 2

Mary: Shalom, Elizabeth —

Elizabeth: Shalom, Mary. The Lord is with you.

(They embrace.)

Mary: And also with you. Oh, Elizabeth, I'm just bursting with news —

Elizabeth: What is it, dear cousin?

Mary: Would you believe I'm going to have a baby?

Elizabeth: *(surprised)* Why — wha — a baby?

Mary: It sounds shocking and incredible I know ... but it's true ... and it's, I believe, — of God!

Elizabeth: Oh, Mary, you are blessed among all women. Zachariah and I thought *we* were blessed being so old but now you say you are pregnant. Oh, Mary. *(hugs Mary)* You know I have this feeling that from your child shall come great things. Tell me all about it!

Mary: Well — it started with an angel —

Elizabeth: An angel? Are you feeling all right Mary? *(jokingly feels Mary's forehead)*

Mary: I'm fine. Seriously, an angel — this presence came over me — he said his name was Gabriel and he said — I was favored and God would overshadow me and I would give birth to the Son of the most high!

Elizabeth: Pretty heady stuff, Mary.

Mary: I know! I'm not sure I understand this. But it's real. And all I could do was sing! I sang that song I learned from mother. *(sings a portion of the Magnificat, using a psalm tone or any musical arrangement that she can handle)* "My soul magnifies the Lord and my spirit rejoices in God my Savior...."

Elizabeth: Wow — as you speak and now as you sing Mary not only have you touched my heart but I just got a kick — a definite movement from *my* little one — Oh, how wonderful —

(Mary and Elizabeth embrace again, then Elizabeth freezes and Mary moves to the previous scene site.)

Scene 3

(Mary resumes her seat near Joseph who unfreezes.)

Mary: So when I told Elizabeth, we both knew something wonderful was going to happen!

Joseph: With the birth of John and now, tonight, *our* son — you were so right, Mary. Now let me tell you *my* angel story.

Mary: Sit close to me, my love, the night air is cool. How's our baby?

Joseph: *(looks at baby)* Fine. *(pauses)* I must admit, I wanted to forget you, Mary — Oh, I loved you but when heard you were pregnant — "Oh no," I thought, "this is wrong, terribly wrong." Then this strange "presence" came to me in the night and I heard words —

Mary: Words like what?

Joseph: Something to this effect — "Don't sweat the pregnancy, Joseph; this is of the Holy Spirit. Take Mary as your wife for she will bear a Son and you are to name him *(whispers for effect)* Jesus!'

Mary: Were you awake or asleep or what?

Joseph: No, I was asleep — it was dreamlike. Then I was told that this Son would be Immanuel — that is — God with us. Can you imagine that?

Mary: I'm surprised and I'm not surprised, Joseph. My, my, we've had wonderful things happen to us, haven't we, love? But it's getting a bit chilly — will you close the stable door, Joseph?

Joseph: *(walks to the side of the stage)* Oh my goodness!

Mary: *(alarmed)* What? What is it?

Joseph: It's a bunch of shepherds coming over the ridge and headed for the alley right toward the stable.

Mary: Maybe some lost sheep.

Joseph: Yes — no — why they're headed right this way.

Mary: Quiet, they'll just pass by.

Joseph: I suppose so. Let's get some rest.

(Music such as a shepherd's carol begins playing.)

The End

**Christmas 1
Cycle B**

Two Futures

Texts: Isaiah 61:10—62:3; Psalm 148; Galatians 4:4-7; Luke 2:22-40

Theme: Parenting and grandparenting

Characters:
  Child
  Person 1
  Person 2

Tone: Thought-provoking

Setting/Props:
  Yo-yo
  Newspaper

Note: The clothing of Person 1 and Person 2 may contrast one another like one dark and one light.

Approximate time: 4-5 minutes

Child: I am only a child, so they say. *(sighs)* I am only a child *(looks at the audience)* you can surely tell. I'm only __(age)__. Soon, though I'll be __(next age)__. Not very old by your standards. Right? Right.
  You know, I'm kinda nervous about the future. What's going to happen to me? But I'm not just nervous about what lies ahead but really kind of excited, too. Ever get butterflies in your stomach? I've got them right now. *(rubs stomach, then giggles nervously)*
  "You're only a child," they say. Yes, and they wonder, as I wonder, will I succeed or fail? Will I have confidence in myself or stay at the bottom like this yo-yo? *(yo-yo spins at the bottom, then when the string is jerked, the yo-yo flies upward)* Will I be afraid of dark places and scary challenges? Will I do well in school? Will I keep the faith that I was taught? Will people listen to me, give me the guidance I want and need? Will the big people support me? Mostly, though, I need what my pastor calls unconditional love, whatever that is I wonder what it's going to be like? *(moves out of the way, but still visible)*

Person 1: Kid looks like me. Ugh. *(glances over at the child)*
Person 2: Bobby looks like me. Wow. *(glances over at the child)*

Person 1: The day he was born, I was at the office signing that million dollar contract I've worked on all month. I sent my secretary with some flowers for my wife. She picked the worst time to have a kid.
Person 2: The day he was born they got me on my cell phone out on the golf course and I got to the hospital just in time. No time for flowers.

Person 1: They told me the kid was all red and like a prune.
Person 2: Babies have their unique appearance when they're born, that's for sure. Beautiful child.

Person 1: Eventually, wife and I decided we'd better get the kid baptized. It's the right thing to do I guess.
Person 2: Soon after he was born, we brought Bobby to church to get him baptized — we wanted to celebrate his new spiritual birth as soon as possible. I'll never forget that morning.

Person 1: I hope he follows my goals and dreams for him.
Person 2: I hope he follows God's leading.

Person 1: "Follow my rules or else," I said over and over again.
Person 2: "Follow the way of truth, child, and you'll do well," I always said.

Person 1: I want him to play baseball — be a pitcher like I was for the Twinkies.
Person 2: My wife and I support him in whatever his gifts, interests, and passions are.

Person 1: Kid never listens.
Person 2: I listen the best I can.

Person 1: I always tried to motivate the kid by telling him he could do a lot better.
Person 2: "Child, you are amazing," I discover day after day.

Person 1: Kid'll get only what he earns or deserves. No more no less. No free lunches in this life. I earned everything I got and I'm proud of it. I did it the old American way. By the sweat of my brow and that's the only way.
Person 2: Life is like getting an undeserved inheritance — of time and opportunity — I hope Bobby discovers that.

Person 1: Wife's parents are a pain. They interfere, give unsolicited advice, and seem pretty controlling.
Person 2: Grandparents are wonderful.

Person 1: Grandma came for a visit last week, spoiled the kid rotten.
Person 2: I'm so glad Grandma visits us. She shares her strong values, her hopes, her dreams, her history, her faith in Christ....

Person 1: Old people are so slow, can't remember things, repeat themselves over and over again — they need to step aside — it's the new millennium, you know.
Person 2: I'm glad for my elders, not only for myself but also for the younger generation. I continue to respect them and learn from them. Perhaps I can be a better parent because of them.

Person 1: *(looks at newspaper)* Seems to be more and more juvenile delinquents....
Person 2: I love reading the school kudos and seeing that our children are doing so well.

Person 1: The television said a kid robbed a convenience story on my block this past week — that's getting too close for comfort.
Person 2: Our neighbor has twins and would you believe they both worked for Habitat for Humanity this past summer on the Indian reservation.

Person 1: I love my child, I really do.
Person 2: I love my child, no question about it.

Person 1: This kid has a 50-50 chance of making a success of himself and I'm crossing my fingers....
Person 2: This child will face many challenges and difficulties in the future but I'm convinced he will make it.

Person 1: I wonder ...
Person 2: I'm confident ...

(Musical interlude.)

The End

Christmas 2
Cycle B

The Adoption

Texts: Jeremiah 31:7-14 (Sirach 24:1-12); Psalm 147:13-21; Ephesians 1:3-14; John 1:(1-9) 10-18

Theme: Adoption, chosen, God's child and God's children

Characters:
　　Dylan (about 12)
　　Dorie (a year older or younger than Dylan)
　　Stagehand (nonspeaking)
　　Mom
　　Dad
　　Uncle Gus Geezer

Tone: Humorous, surprising

Setting/Props:
　　Drinking glass
　　Sign that reads "Last Christmas"
　　The first setting is in the children's bedroom and the second setting is around a table decorated with Christmas ornaments. The third scene is anywhere in the house.

Approximate time: 5-6 minutes

Scene 1

Dylan: Dorie, did you hear what I heard? *(has a drinking glass in his hand that was used to listen through the bedroom wall)*

Dorie: No, what — snoopy-doopy nosey-posey?

Dylan: I'm not nosey — just curious.

Dorie: Well ...

Dylan: Mom and Dad are going to get a new "family" member!

Dorie: What makes you think that? Mom is through having kids.

Dylan: Well, in low tones, like they do after we've gone to bed — I heard Mom — your mother and mine, Elsie Schubble, say, "Pete, let's use the extra room." And I heard Dad through this amazing through-the-wall-megaphone *(holds up glass)* grumble about "the expense of it all."

Dorie: Oh, boy. I've got it. It's an animal. They're getting us a pet. Finally, after all these years of begging for a dalmation or a Siamese cat or ...

Dylan: *(interrupts)* No, it's got to be a big animal. We have ten acres out here in the country you know. And I heard Dad say something about $8,000-10,000. That's no dog, no cat, no hamster, no ...

Dorie: *(interrupts)* Then I've got it. It's a kangaroo.

Dylan: A kangaroo? Are you nuts?

Dorie: *(excitedly)* No, Dylan, I read it in the paper. The zoo over in Fordsville has an abundance of kangaroos. They're going to sell off five of them next week.

Dylan: I don't think so, Dorie. I think they're going to surprise us with an Arabian horse or something exotic like a llama or a pair of ostriches. Maybe a buffalo or a baby elephant.

Dorie: Ha, ha, oh sure. *(sarcastically)* Anybody want to buy some ostrich eggs? Have an egg for breakfast and you won't have to eat until next Tuesday.

Dylan: Whatever it is — it'll be fun. I'd settle for a nice black Lab. Plenty of room to romp here in the country.

Dorie: Yeah, cool.

Dylan: Oh no! *(grabs head as if in great pain)*

Dorie: What is it, Dylan? What's the matter?

Dylan: What if it isn't an animal but a person Mom and Dad are bringing into *our* home? Could they be planning to use the spare bedroom for crazy Uncle Gus?

Dorie: Our Uncle Gus Geezer? You think so?

Dylan: Uncle Gus is Mom's only brother — and he's not that well —

Dorie: Oh no! Remember last Christmas?

Scene 2
(Stagehand walks by carrying a sign that reads, "Last Christmas")

Mom: I'm so glad you could join us, Gus, for Christmas dinner this year.

Dad: You're always welcome here, right, kids?

Dylan and Dorie: *(give mock assent)* Yes, Merry Christmas, Uncle Gus.

Uncle Gus: *(talks like a butler still on duty — stiff accent, eccentric movements)* Thank you, ma'am, thank you, sir. Merry Christmas to you, Dylan Robert and Dorie Kay. It is extremely kind of you to invite me to your Christmas festivities. I must admit, though I am fully self-sufficient, that it is quite lonely in my apartment since my hasty "retirement." By the way, the tea was a bit tepid — the turkey too dry. The napkins belong on the right side of the plate, and do you ever dust, sister? I noticed a bit of dust in and amongst the knickknacks that you have collected over there on the hutch. Oh, pardon me, I still think I'm on duty. *(fakes a laugh)*

Dad: Do you miss your work, Gus?

Uncle Gus: Being a butler for Mrs. Chadworth was fine until I was prematurely retired. No reason at all 'cept I redecorated the entire mansion while Mrs. Chadworth was in Europe for the summer. Apparently, she didn't like my color scheme — purple and green.

Mom: Well, brother dear, we love having you — what are your plans for the future?

(Dylan and Dorie look at one another and shudder.)

Uncle Gus: Guess I just have to become a tutor to my niece and nephew and train them in good manners. I noticed they are quite deficient in that area. *(sarcastically)* How long have you lived in the ghetto?

Dylan and Dorie: *(look smitten)* We weren't, Uncle Gus ... *(laugh nervously)*

Uncle Gus: I noticed you dress in trendy clothes — be careful or you'll look like gang members.

Mom: *(changes subject)* Well, Merry Christmas, Gus.

Dad: And have a happy New Year! Let's all sing a Christmas carol.

(All sing "Deck The Halls.")

Scene 3

Dylan: Do you really think Uncle Geezer will be invited to live here?

Dorie: I'd rather have a pet animal any day — even a lizard or a snake but not Uncle Gus Geezer. How could Mom be so neat and her blood brother such an out-and-out geek?

Dylan: Dunno. What are we going to do? Here come the folks. They said they had something important to tell us. *(groans)*

(Dad and Mom appear.)

Dad and Mom: Good morning, kids. We have something exciting to share with you.

Mom: Dad and I have been discussing it for a long time.

Dylan: *(slyly)* We're going to Disney World?

Dorie: *(mockingly)* We're getting a satellite dish? A cell phone for each of us?

Dylan: Could it be ...

Mom: *(interrupts)* You'll never guess. We are going to fill the extra family room.

Dorie: With what? A thing or an animal, I hope, or a person?

Mom: Not a thing.

Dad: Not an animal.

Dylan: Oh no, there goes my black Lab.

Dorie: And my kangaroo.

Dylan: A person! Oh no, not Uncle Gus! *(covers head with pillow)*

Dorie: Uncle Gus. Yikes. *(runs out of the room but quickly returns)*

Mom: No, no. Where did you get those ideas?

Dorie: Well, Dylan overheard you say something about the spare room and the cost of whatever ...

Mom: *(interrupts)* Oh no, we're going to adopt a child. You're going to have a baby sister or a new baby brother, isn't that exciting?

Dylan: Adopt?

Dorie: Adopt, we never thought of that. Wow! Wowee!

Dad: And this child will have all the privileges and opportunities that you two kids have had. Freedom, education, love, and a future. How do you feel about all that?

Dorie: Relieved.

Dylan: Yeah, relieved and thankful.

The End

Additional Worship Sketches

Synopses Of The Additional Worship Sketches

Better To Be A "Lert"

We meet two different kinds of humanoids. One group is called the Nods and the other group is called the Lerts. The Nods are careless and inattentive and as a result suffer a tragedy. The Lerts on the other hand are attentive, watchful, and enjoy their life. The question that surfaces is, "Who does one relate to in this Advent season?"

The Will

A widely separated family must live together in order to inherit the family mansion. This idea is based on an idea by F. Scott Fitzgerald as found among his papers after he died.

The Rabbi's Gift

A famous monastery falls on hard times. The remaining monks are downcast and sad. The abbot goes to visit an old rabbi whose hut is nearby at the edge of the forest and inquires about direction and wisdom. The old rabbi announces a mysterious, but powerful, message: "The Messiah is among you." The abbot takes this message back to his bickering, depressed brothers and the message changes everyone's attitude and bickering view of one another. The monastery once again becomes an attractive, happy place. This sketch was influenced by Francis Duff's story titled "The Rabbi's Gift."

Watching For "A Coming"

Several people — a waiting man, husband and wife, mother and teenager — are waiting and watching for someone at the airport. After intertwining discussions, the waiting man announces he is waiting for a prince who comes disguised. All are amused and surprised, hardly believing the waiting man.

Children's Advent Sketch

Better To Be A "Lert"

Theme: Be watchful and alert for Christ's coming

Characters:
    Narrator 1
    Nod 1
    Nod 2
    Nod 3
    Nod 4
    FEMA Agent (nonspeaking)
    Narrator 2
    Lert 1
    Lert 2
    Lert 3
    Lert 4
    Offstage Voice 1
    Offstage Voice 2

Tone: Humorous, cautionary

Setting/Props:
    Ball
    Book
    Large "elephant-sized" ears
    Flappers

Approximate time: 6-7 minutes

(Music, such as a lullaby, plays in the background.)

Narrator 1: Once upon a time, there lived a clan of humanlike creatures who had some rather unusual physical and mental features. The people of Nod had bodies like yours and mine in many ways. Their heads, trunks, legs, and arms were normal-looking, although admittedly, they did have very large elephant-like ears.

(Nods show themselves off — demonstrating poses as would a ballet dancer, a weight lifter, or a model.)

Narrator 1: Two other features that were distinctly different from humanoids was that they had very squinty eyes. They would peer through them like they were watching through slits in a screen. And instead of hands, they had flappers. Their flappers were very useful and very necessary for their livelihood.

(Nods show and demonstrate flappers as hands.)

Nod 1: See, when I'm happy, I clap with my flappers. *(demonstrates clapping)*

Nod 2: When I'm hot and sweaty, I use my flappers to cool off. *(demonstrates waving flapper to cool off)*

Nod 3: Hello there. When I'm hungry, I sit down to a sumptuous meal and I shovel it in like this. *(demonstrates shoveling food into mouth)*

Nod 4: When I go for a swim in the ocean or the pool, I paddle, paddle, paddle. *(demonstrates paddling in the water)*

All Nods: And when we worship, we pray. *(demonstrate putting flappers together in prayerful gesture)*

Narrator 1: These humanoids from the Land of Nod loved using their flappers. They worked with their flappers.

(Nods demonstrate working.)

Narrator 1: They played with their flappers.

(Nods toss a ball among themselves.)

Narrator 1: And most of all — they used their flappers as tappers. By tapping any object, they could understand it. By tapping another person, they could communicate in secret code.

(Nods tap each other.)

Narrator 1: By tapping a book, they could comprehend it in a few seconds.

(Nods tap a book.)

Narrator 1: You see, the people of Nod were brilliant, unusually intelligent, and sensitive. But, unfortunately, they did have one flaw. Quite without warning, they would nod off and fall sound asleep!

(Nods fall asleep, wake each other up, and fall promptly to sleep again.)

Narrator 1: Oh, they were geniuses. But their attention spans were *soooo* short and their memories were, unfortunately, shorter, yet. One day, a representative from FEMA (Federal Emergency Management Agency) arrived and unveiled the government's plan to mobilize the people for evacuation. You see, a dangerous volcano above the Land of Nod was acting up again. But as the FEMA agent spoke to the citizens of Nod about the impending danger, they nodded off for several twenty- to thirty-second siestas. Consequently, they missed the details of the evacuation.

(FEMA Agent enters and pantomimes talking to the Nods, who keep falling asleep. The FEMA Agent finishes speaking and exits.)

Narrator 1: I'm sorry to report that history has it that because the people of Nod nodded off too often and too long, tragedy overtook them and they disappeared from the face of the earth.

(Narrator 1 sits down and Narrator 2 stands and speaks.)

Narrator 2: I have a story to tell, also — a happier story — about the cousins of the people of Nod. These folks lived in the Land of Lert. They, too, looked like humanoids — had larger ears, squinty eyes, and flappers for hands. But they did not use their flappers as tappers like their cousins. The Lerts used their flappers as clappers. And they were very attentive and very vigilant. The Lerts applauded everything.

(All Lerts applaud.)

Lert 1: *(to other Lerts)* Good morning, my fellow Lerts.

(All Lerts applaud.)

Lert 2: What a wonderful crowd here today watching this sketch.

(All Lerts applaud.)

Lert 3: It's been a beautiful day, hasn't it?

(All Lerts applaud.)

Lert 4: Good evening to you, too.

(All Lerts applaud.)

Offstage Voice 1: Avon calling — Avon calling.

(All Lerts smile and applaud.)

Offstage Voice 2: Domino's Pizza. Twelve-incher with cheese and pepperoni!

(All Lerts applaud.)

Offstage Voice 1: Time to get up out of bed and go to school.

(All Lerts applaud.)

Offstage Voice 2: Time to go to church and worship.

(All Lerts applaud.)

Narrator 2: Everyone felt affirmed and appreciated in the Land of Lert. You could cough and what would they do, these silly fellows? You guessed it — of course — they would applaud.

(Narrator 2 coughs and all Lerts applaud.)

Narrator 2: And one day, when the FEMA agent came to the land of Lert to warn them of the impending flood from heavy rains in the mountains, they listened *very carefully* to the evacuation plans. They clapped with their flappers and they listened and they heard every word and memorized every important detail — and when the flood came, inundating the valley and destroying everything in its path, the people from the Land of Lert were safe. And they laughed and clapped at the flood, knowing its water could never harm nor frighten them. In this Advent season, there is a moral for all who would heed this Advent sketch. The moral is, "Don't be a *Nod*, but be a *Lert*."

The End

Worship Sketch

The Will

Theme: The challenge of living together in community, love one another

Characters:
- Attorney
- Carl (brother to Jen and Merrial)
- Jen (sister number 1)
- Merrial (sister number 2)
- Receptionist

Tone: Argumentative with a surprise at the end

Setting/Props:
- Desk
- Telephone
- Intercom
- Chairs
- Nail file
- Gum
- Scene 1 takes place in a lawyer's office
- Scene 2 takes place in the law office reception room

Approximate time: 7-8 minutes

Scene 1
(Attorney is sitting at his desk. The telephone rings and he answers it.)

Attorney: Delbeck Law Office, Attorney Johnson speaking, how may I help you? Oh, it's you, Frank. Thanks for getting back to me — no, my lunch hour is over — no problem. What did you find out? *(listens to conversation at the other end)* Huh, mmm. Oh, really? That's interesting — most interesting — you mean for the Farges family — Carl, Jen, and Merrial? Really? *(laughs heartily)* That ought to be interesting, especially when you know the family like I do. They grew up around here. I know them very well. The probate is finished. Okay. And I'm to inform the Farges family of the results? Okay — well, thanks, Frank. I'll get right on it. Oh, boy. *(to receptionist on intercom)* Tell the Farges folks that I'll be with them in fifteen minutes or so.

Scene 2
(In the law firm's reception room. Receptionist is seated at a desk and Jen is sitting in a chair, filing her nails and rapidly chewing gum. Carl enters.)

Carl: Hello, Jen — long time no see.

Jen: *(coolly)* Hello, yourself, Carl. What's this meeting all about? And what for?

Carl: What do you mean?

Jen: Well, coming 1,000 miles to this crummy lawyer's office.

Carl: Dunno.

Jen: You don't know, either? Is this some mystery?

Carl: Maybe Merrial knows. She should be here any minute now. *(paces the floor, sits down, then gets up again several times)*

Jen: *(attempts to make conversation even though it's a bit awkward)* Well, you still working for that politician? Right-winger, isn't he?

Carl: Yeah, I'm still working for him. Why shouldn't I? Been eight years now and we'll get him elected governor, yet.

Jen: Too conservative. Squeaks, he's so straight. I'd never vote for him.

Carl: Well, at least he's not going to fall for your crowd and their liberal crap.

Jen: Liberal? At least I have an open mind about a few things. You've so conservative you're to the right of Genghis Khan. Listen, Carl, just because a *person* thinks a little bit that doesn't make him a way-out-in-left-field liberal. Oh, Carl, you've never changed one iota since we graduated from high school.

Carl: *(angrily)* Why should I? Just because you're so wishy-washy on anything that's important.

Jen: Oh, shut up.

Carl: You know, Jen, I don't shut up, I grow up, and when I look at you, Jen, Jen, Jen, my dearest, older sister *(sarcastically)*, I *throw up!*

(Carl and Jen glare at one another for a while.)

Jen: *(sighs)* Let's face it, we've never gotten along and I see we never will — good thing we live in different states. Oh, here comes Merrial. Look at that, will you?

(Merrial arrives dressed in an extremely simple dress reminiscent of a "flower child" from the late '60s and early '70s.)

Merrial: Hello, Jen — Carl. How are you? What's this meeting about, anyway?

Carl: Hello, Merrial. I don't really know. The attorney called me here and said to bring my siblings — that's you two — Merrial, the strange one, and Jen, here, the sharp-tongued one.

Jen: Stop it, Carl — Hello, Merrial. Let's try to get along at least until this mystery meeting is over. Apparently it's something important we must attend to.

Carl: *(tries to be civil)* Okay, okay. *(to Merrial)* And what have you been doing since we saw you at the family gathering in the summer of '89?

Merrial: Well, I've been working with Greenpeace, trying to save the whales, the pandas in China, and now we're working to do something drastic about the declining rain forests in Central America.

Carl: Still the do-gooder, aren't you, Merrial? Any liberal cause — there's Merrial. Saving everybody and everything but yourself, right?

Merrial: I resent that! What are you getting at?

Jen: Well, why didn't you save your marriage? That was going extinct. Why didn't you save your money? Poof! Away it went — every dime.

Carl: And what about all this simple living stuff? Next you'll be living in a cult of some kind.

Merrial: *(defensively)* I live a simple lifestyle because I am a citizen of the world. I don't believe in this parochial, narrow, nationalism stuff. Maybe you do, but not me.

Carl: Social sister of mine! That's what you are, Merrial.

Receptionist: Mr. Delbeck will be with you in five minutes. May I get you something to drink? I have coffee, tea, and soda.

Jen: *(angrily)* No! *(changes demeanor)* Oh yes, I'll have a soda. Make it a Dr Pepper.

Carl: Coffee for me, ma'am.

Merrial: Herbal tea is fine. *(sweetly)* Thank you. Now what did you call me, Carl? A socialist what?

Jen: Oh, how could our parents hatch such different kids? It's incredible. You'd think we were born on different planets. We don't even agree on religion.

Carl: I'm a fundamentalist and I'm proud of it. Black is black and white is white, in my book. I'm sick of these people who run around and preach, "Everything is gray."

Merrial: You Christians can't get along. I'm glad I switched to New Age religion. At least one can experience God within oneself and not all this dogma and doctrine malarkey.

Jen: I'm too busy for that religion stuff — leave me out of it. Too many hypocrites. Oh, here's the attorney.

(Attorney enters and shakes hands with the siblings.)

Attorney: Hello, folks — Carl Farge? Jennifer Farge? And you must be Merrial. I'm pleased to meet you. I'm sorry for this short notice, but I had to follow the stipulations of the will.

Carl, Jen, and Merrial: The will? What will?

Attorney: Oh, your Great Aunt Martha named you three as heirs of her seaside mansion near Cape Cod.

Carl, Jen, and Merrial: She did?

Attorney: She did. It's worth three million dollars.

Carl, Jen, and Merrial: Wow! Whoa, whew! I can't believe this. It's like hitting the lottery.

Attorney: But there is one stipulation that your Great Aunt Martha made ...

Carl: *(interrupts)* And what is that? I'm sure it'll be no problem.

Jen: No problem.

Merrial: No problem.

Attorney: Your Great Aunt Martha stipulates that in order for you to receive the mansion, you three must *live* in it!

Carl, Jen, and Merrial: *(shocked)* Live in it? Together?

(Lights fade.)

The End

Christmas Worship Sketch

The Rabbi's Gift

Theme: Jesus among you

Characters:
    Sexton
    Monk 1
    Monk 2
    Rabbi
    Abbot

Tone: Thoughtful

Setting/Props:
    CD or tape of "Chant" by Benedictine monks
    Door
    Table
    Chairs
    Large Bible
    Monks habits (optional)

Approximate time: 10-12 minutes

Sexton: Good day. My name is Abelard. I am the sexton here at St. Dominic's monastery. My job is to take care of things. What things, you ask? Why, things like tolling the tower bell, tending to the candlewicks in the chapel, and caring for the details of the cemetery like the burials and the grave diggings. I've been a sexton here in this place for almost eighty years now. It's my job and it's also my home. Once, long ago, this monastery, St. Dominic's of Vientia, was such a happy nurturing place ... *(fades away)*

(Monks in garb laugh, chant, play, and pray. Chanting music is heard in the background. Monks go into freeze positions. Chants fade away.)

Sexton: But hard times came and things went from bad to worse. Only a handful of old monks shuffled through the cloister halls. I remember the prayers and songs at matins and vespers were so sad.

(Monks unfreeze and shuffle about with their heads down. They chant only halfheartedly, argue and fight with one another, and eventually isolate themselves from each other. Monks go into freeze position.)

Sexton: Now, nearby the monastery woods, there lived an old Jewish rabbi. The rabbi visited his hut in the woods from time to time, to fast and to pray.

(Monks unfreeze and two Monks talk among themselves.)

Monk 1: I see the old rabbi is back.

Monk 2: Yes, he is. That's *his* business, I guess — none of ours.

Monk 1: Never talks, does he?

Monk 2: Nope. But pass the word to the other brothers: "The rabbi walks in the woods."

Monk 1: You know, even though things are bad here at the monastery, I feel good, for some reason, when he is around. I don't understand it.

Monk 2: Me, too — strange, isn't it? And we don't even know him.

(Monks freeze.)

Sexton: One day, our abbot decided to visit the rabbi. So, after matins, he took off down the path to the edge of the woods.

(Abbot walks toward door. As Sexton reads the following lines, Abbot and Rabbi act them out.)

Sexton: And as the abbot approached the door to the hut where the rabbi lived, the rabbi stepped out to meet him with outstretched arms, and welcomed him like he had been waiting for him to come for a long, long time. They hugged one another like long-lost brothers — and then just stood smiling at each other for the longest time. Then they went inside the rabbi's little hovel.

(Abbot and Rabbi sit down at a table, open a large, large Bible, and then Rabbi begins to cry. And soon Abbot joins him, weeping. The two sit crying until the tears no longer come, then they sit quietly.)

Rabbi: I sense that you and your brothers at St. Dominic's are serving God with heavy hearts. And it appears that you have come to visit with me and to ask a teaching of me.

Abbot: Yes, my friend. It has been some time now that we have labored without peace. What teaching do you have?

Rabbi: I will give you a teaching, but you can only repeat it once. After that, no one must ever say it aloud again. Agree?

Abbot: *(holds hand over heart)* Yes, yes, I will honor your request.

Rabbi: *(looks straight into Abbot's eyes)* This is what I have to say to you *(pauses)*, "The Messiah is among you."

(There is a long, quiet pause.)

Sexton: For some time it was quiet in the little hut. Neither the abbot nor the rabbi spoke again except for the rabbi to say,

Rabbi: You must go now. God's peace to you.

Sexton: The abbot got up, walked out of the rabbi's hut with the words, "The Messiah is among you," burning in his heart.

(Abbot departs.)

Sexton: Early the next morning, before matins, the abbot called a meeting of his brother monks.

(Monks gather around Abbot.)

Abbot: Yesterday, my brothers, I received a teaching from "The rabbi who walks in the woods." He said he was aware of our pain and struggles and that this teaching was never again to be spoken aloud. *(pauses)* It is this: The rabbi said *(pauses)* that one of us is the Messiah.

Sexton: Well, the Monks were amazed, to say the least. Their jaws dropped and their eyes got big. And listen ...

Monks: *(unfreeze and all talk at once among themselves)* What does this mean, that one of us is the Messiah? Is Brother John the Messiah? Or Brother Nathaniel or Father Damian or Brother Thomas? Am I the Messiah? Are you the Messiah? What could this mean?

(Monks freeze.)

Sexton: Even though they were puzzled by the rabbi's teaching, after that morning no one ever mentioned it again. And after a few weeks, I noticed something. While I tended to my sexton duties, the brothers began to treat one another differently.

(Monks unfreeze.)

Monk 1: You before me, sir —

Monk 2: Oh, thank you, Brother Martin, God bless you.

Monk 1: That's quite all right.

Monk 2: By the way, Brother Martin, do you want to go to vespers with me and offer our praises to the Lord?

Monk 1: Oh yes, what a privilege to chant with you and the other brothers like we used to do.

(Monks chant happily together, embrace one another, and dance.)

Sexton: There was a new, gentle, loving spirit like long ago. These brothers lived as though they had found something in each other they had never seen before. Oh, their songs were quite beautiful. Their prayers were awesome and visitors came again from far and wide. They were nourished and uplifted and left inspired. St. Dominic's monastery flourished like a flower in spring. And the rabbi? Well, he disappeared — never walked the woods again, but the monks who heard his teaching felt warmed by the memory of his presence.

The End

Advent Worship Sketch

Watching For A "Coming"

Theme: Incarnation, God comes hidden in disguise

Characters:
- Ticket Agent
- Waiting Man
- Husband
- Wife
- Mother
- Teenager

Tone: Puzzling until the end

Setting/Props: Airport lobby

Approximate time: 6-8 minutes

(Waiting Man is standing at the ticket counter talking to Ticket Agent.)

Ticket Agent: You found what you are looking for, sir?

Waiting Man: Oh yes, in a most surprising but logical place.

Ticket Agent: And where was that?

Waiting Man: *(a bit embarrassed)* I found my wallet with my identification, my credit cards, even all my cash, right where it had dropped out — in the men's restroom — by the stool.

Ticket Agent: Well, good for you, sir — now you can at least identify yourself officially when he comes.

Waiting Man: Yeah, it would be pretty embarrassing otherwise.

Ticket Agent: His plane will land on runway number two.

Waiting Man: Oh, thanks, where exactly is runway two?

Ticket Agent: You can see it through that window in the north bay.

Waiting Man: Okay, I'll watch from here.

(Scene shifts to a Husband and Wife standing in airport lobby.)

Husband: Do you see him?

Wife: No, what does he look like?

Husband: Only talked to him on the phone. He said he'd meet us here in the airport lobby — would be wearing an L. L. Bean blue turtleneck.

Wife: I still don't know why mother couldn't visit us this weekend.

Husband: We've gone over that before, hush now.

Wife: You're stressed, I know.

Husband: Three company break-ins in six months — wouldn't *you* be stressed?

Wife: *(talks about the earlier subject — her mother's coming)* But Mom would be no problem — she's so self-sufficient.

Husband: *(preoccupied with his subject — the company break-ins)* And no insurance to cover the cost.

Wife: She'd only stay a year or two.

Husband: Better late than never to do something about it. Where is that security salesman? I'm going to tell him I want cyclone fences, pit bull dogs, and even a moat with crocodiles in it if this guy can deliver it.

Wife: Just kidding — Mom only stays a week at a time — you know that.

Husband: If this salesman can promise and deliver security for my business — you can bet he's got the contract. *(impatiently)* Oh, where is he anyway?

Mother: *(to Husband and Wife)* Pardon me, I overheard you talking, sir. You're looking for someone in a blue turtleneck sweater, aren't you? I saw such a person out in the parking lot when I just came in. He'll be coming this way.

Husband: Why, thank you, that's very kind of you. And *who* are you watching for — maybe we can return the favor?

Mother: My son! He's coming home from St. Olaf today or tomorrow — didn't say which day nor by which means of transportation —

Husband: You mean, he didn't tell you?

Mother: No, I just got the last half of his message on my answering machine. I heard, "Garble, garble ... so, Mom, pick me up at the terminal. Love you. 'Bye." And look at me, supermom, running from the bus station to the train station and here to the airport, just so I can welcome him properly. Haven't seen him for a year. Oh, dear ...

Husband: *(interrupts)* You're feeling quiet frustrated, aren't you?

Mother: Yes, yes, of course.

Husband: Do you want my advice?

Mother: No, no, no advice — just a listening ear — and some sympathy — well, okay, I am a bit curious. What is your advice?

Husband: Stay home — quit running around. He'll call you. You can't watch three places at once.

Mother: Oh, I guess you're right. I'll go home and wait for his call. That makes more sense. Thank you, sir, thank you very much.

(Scene shifts back to the ticket counter.)

Ticket Agent: Patience, boy, patience. Who are you looking for?

Teenager: The Rapper, of course. Didn't you read about him?

Ticket Agent: You mean the lead in that new rock band from Dallas?

Teenager: Yeah, man, the Rapper Dapper from Dallas. He's awesome. I have every CD the Rapper and his group ever made. Now I'm gonna see 'em in person if he ever comes.

Ticket Agent: Well, watch the lobby door, Flight 602 comes in on that side of the terminal. And good luck. I hope you recognize him.

Teenager: Cool, man. *(to Waiting Man)* And *who* exactly is it that *you* are watching and waiting for? Peter, Paul, and Mary, old man? *(laughs)*

Waiting Man: Well, no, son, that's my era and my kind of music, but ...

Teenager: *(interrupts)* Fats Domino? Elvis Presley? Elvis is alive, you know.

Waiting Man: *(laughs)* So they say. Actually, I'm waiting for ... ah ... ah ... I know you'll find this hard to believe, but I'm waiting and watching for a ... a... prince.

All: *(turn their heads toward Waiting Man after hearing this)* A what?

Waiting Man: A ... a ... prince! Prince Savero from Monte Carlino. I'm the official greeter from the governor's office and my job is to spot him, greet him, and wine and dine him — even though he comes, they say, in disguise. They say I'll know him ... when I see him ... at least, I hope so.

The End

Outdoor Nativity Backdrop Set

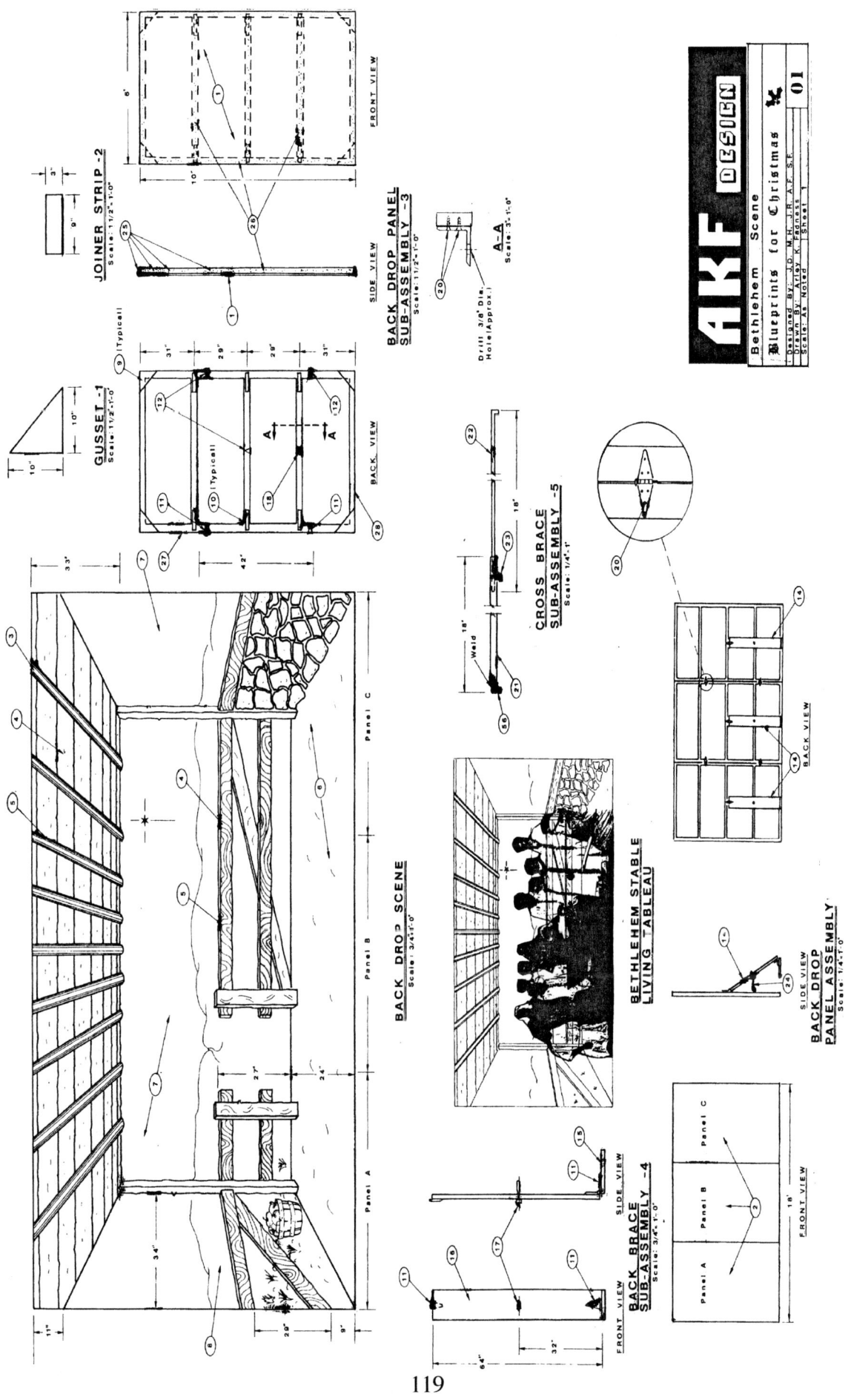

Materials List

Item	Description	Quantity	Blueprint No.
1	muslin cloth	as required	01
2	light neutral flat latex paint	as required	01
3	medium brown paint	as required	01
4	light brown paint	as required	01
5	black paint (for accent)	as required	01
6	beige paint	as required	01
7	light blue paint	as required	01
8	light green paint	as required	01
9	1/2" plywood gusset -1	12	01
10	1/2" plywood joiner strip -2	18	01
11	1/2" x 6" strap hinge - right	10	01
12	1/2" x 6" strap hinge - left	10	01
13	backdrop panel sub-assembly -3	3	01
14	back brace sub-assembly -4	3	01
15	1" x 10" x 13" wood base	3	01
16	1" x 10" x 5' - 4" wood base	3	01
17	1/4" x 1" eye bolt	3	01
18	2" x 2" angle iron	3	01
19	#7 nails or equivalent	as required	01
20	#8 wood screws or equivalent	as required	01
21	3/8" x 18" pipe	3	01
22	3/8" x 18" rod	3	01
23	5/16" set screw	3	01
24	cross brace sub-assembly -5	3	01
25	3/8" staples	as required	01
26	wheat paste or equivalent	as required	01
27	1" x 4" x 10' pine board	6	01
28	1" x 4" x 6' pine board	15	01
29	1/2" x 24" diameter plywood base -6	1 per unit	02
30	8" diameter metal can weight -7	1 per unit	02
31	1 1/3" diameter x 6" pipe	1 per unit	02
32	cement	as required	02
33	1 1/4" x 40" wood dowel	as required	02
34	1 1/4 " x 6' wood dowel	as required	02
35	1 1/4" x 4" screw	1	02
36	1/4" wing nut	1	02
37	eye screw	2	02
38	weight light standard sub-assembly -8	1 per unit	02
39	7.40" diameter x 14" cylindrical housing	1 per unit	02
40	7.50" ± diameter sheet metal circular	1 per unit	02
41	1/8" x 1" x 24.22" iron light hanger	1 per unit	02
42	lamp socket	1 per unit	02
43	spot lamp	1 per unit	02
44	gel holder -9	3 per unit	02
45	dimmer switch	4 per unit	02
46	duplex outlet	5 per unit	02
47	#14 wire	as required	02
48	electrical connectors	7	02
49	electrical cap	1	02
50	600 amp cord and 3-prong plug	1	02
51	1/2" x 8" x 20" plywood board	4 per unit	02
52	1 1/2" hinge	2 per unit	02
53	wood screws	as required	02
54	control box sub-assembly -10	1	02
55	puppet theater (options) -11		02
56	3/8" x 4" rod	3	01
57	spotlight sub-assembly -12	2	02
58	"C" clamp	2	02
59	wire or strong tie	as required	02
	luminary (optional)	as required	02

Construction Notes #01
Bethehem Stable Scene Backdrop

1. Build five panels as per Blueprint #01
    a. Fold muslin cloth over ends
    b. Glue dotted areas and staple
    c. Allow glue to dry
2. Paint two coats light latex
3. Hinge panels together
4. Install back braces
5. Paint stable backdrop as specified
6. Position people, props, and animals

Construction And Setup Notes For Drawings A Through N

1. Figures for the collections of Drawings A through N may be made out of 1-inch by 4-inch pine boards ripped into 1-inch by 2-inch slats and/or 1-inch by 6-inch boards ripped into 1-inch by 3-inch slats. Also, one-half-inch thick plywood may be used for other figures such as the sheep. Figures may be painted in fluorescent colors or other colors in order to enhance the visual effect desired.

2. The crèche scene pictured in Drawing A uses figures on Drawings B through N. The scene pictures the construction of the stable with some of the principles included, assuming the other figures are further away. See photos 1 and 2.

3. A crèche scene using figures on Drawings F, G, and H, may be set up as a more simple indoor or outdoor scene. See photo 3. These figures may be painted white if using a dark background. Spotlights will accent the scene beautifully.

Note: Several figures of Drawings A through N are adaptations of an original unknown source. Sketches and dimensions are copyrighted © by Arley K. Fadness, 2007.

4' x 1/4" WIDE SLATS
PAINTED FLUORESCENT
COLORS. 14 (TYP.)
SPOT LIGHTS MAY BE
USED.

Nativity Outdoor Scene — A

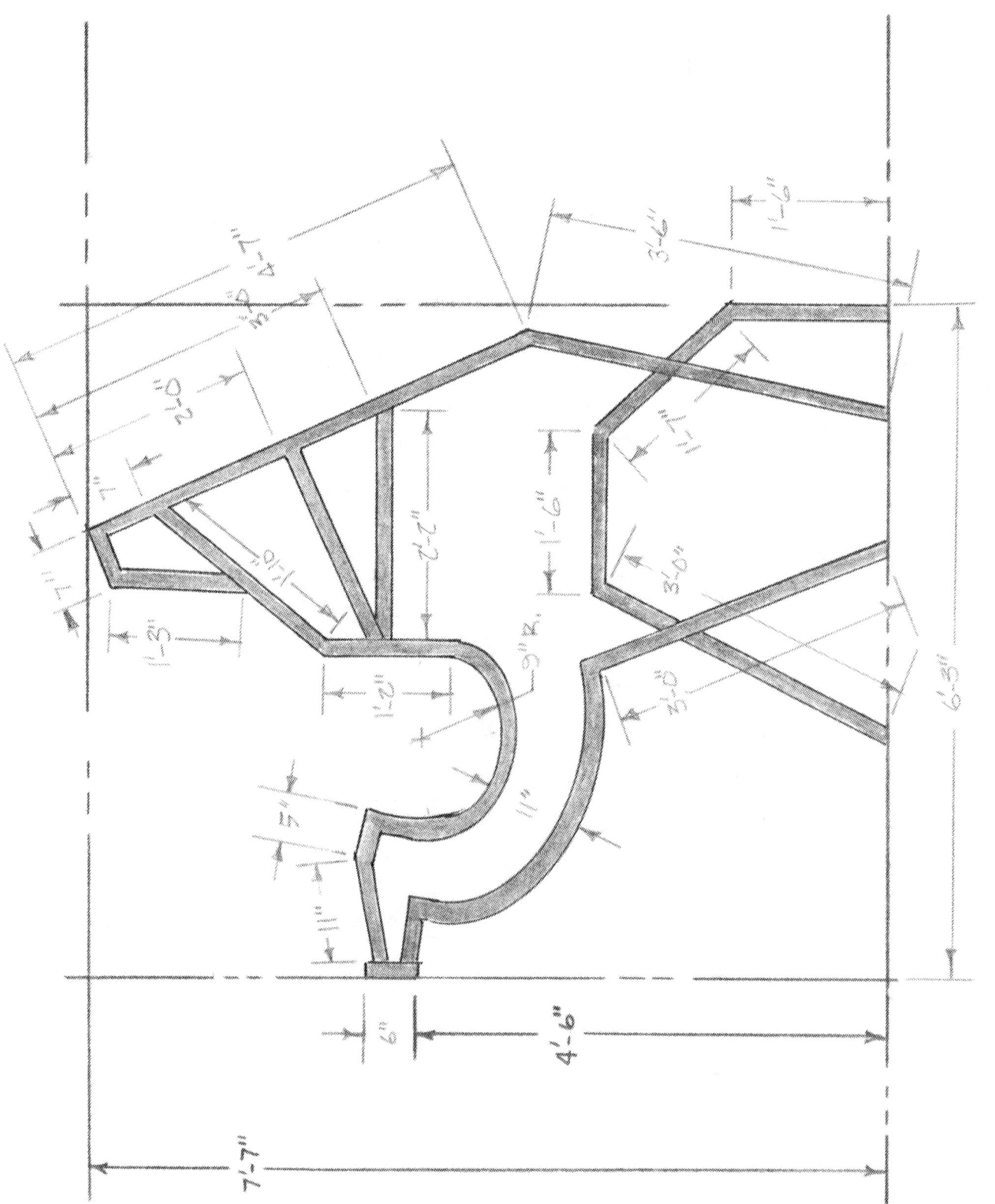

Wise Man On Camel — B

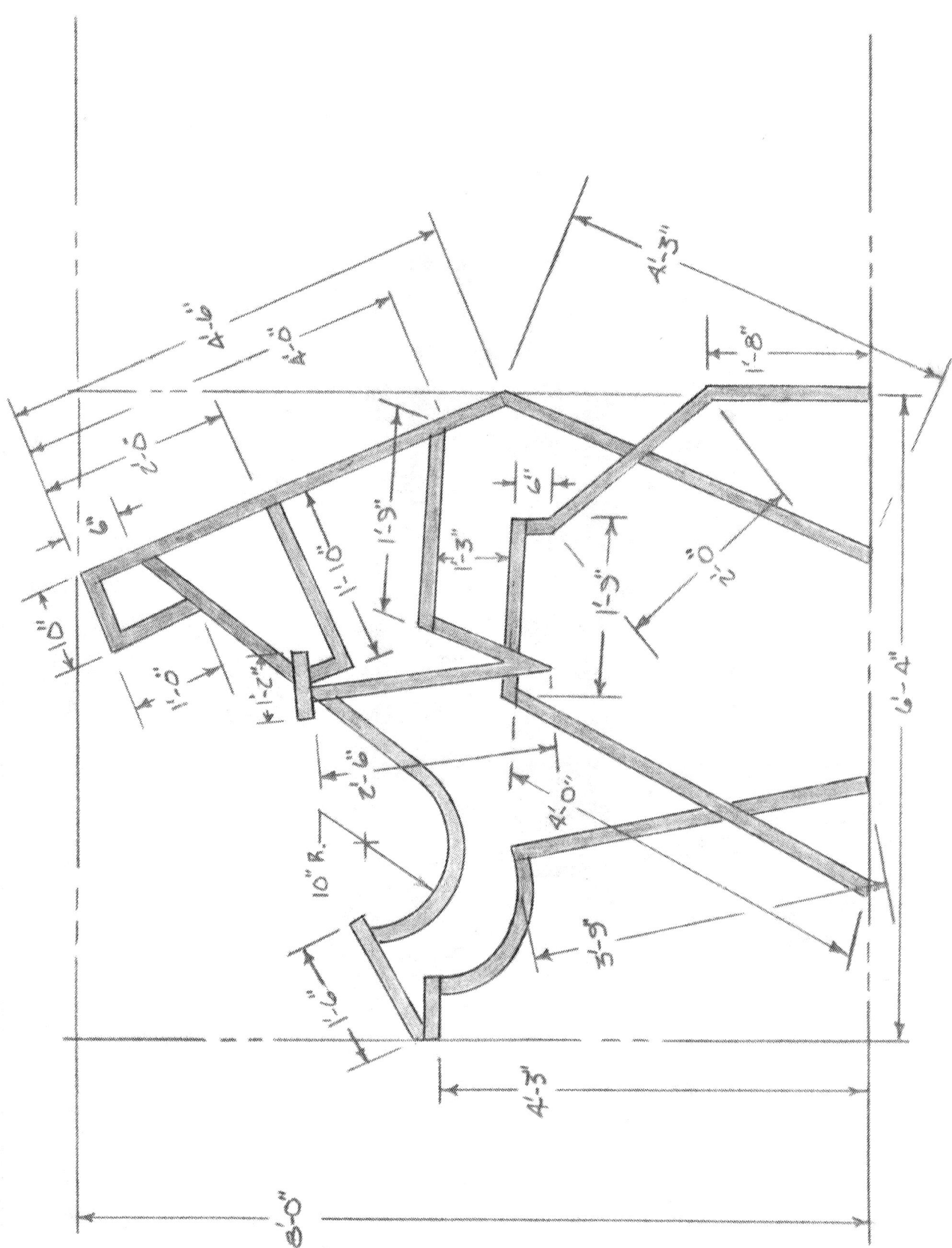

Wise Man On Camel — C

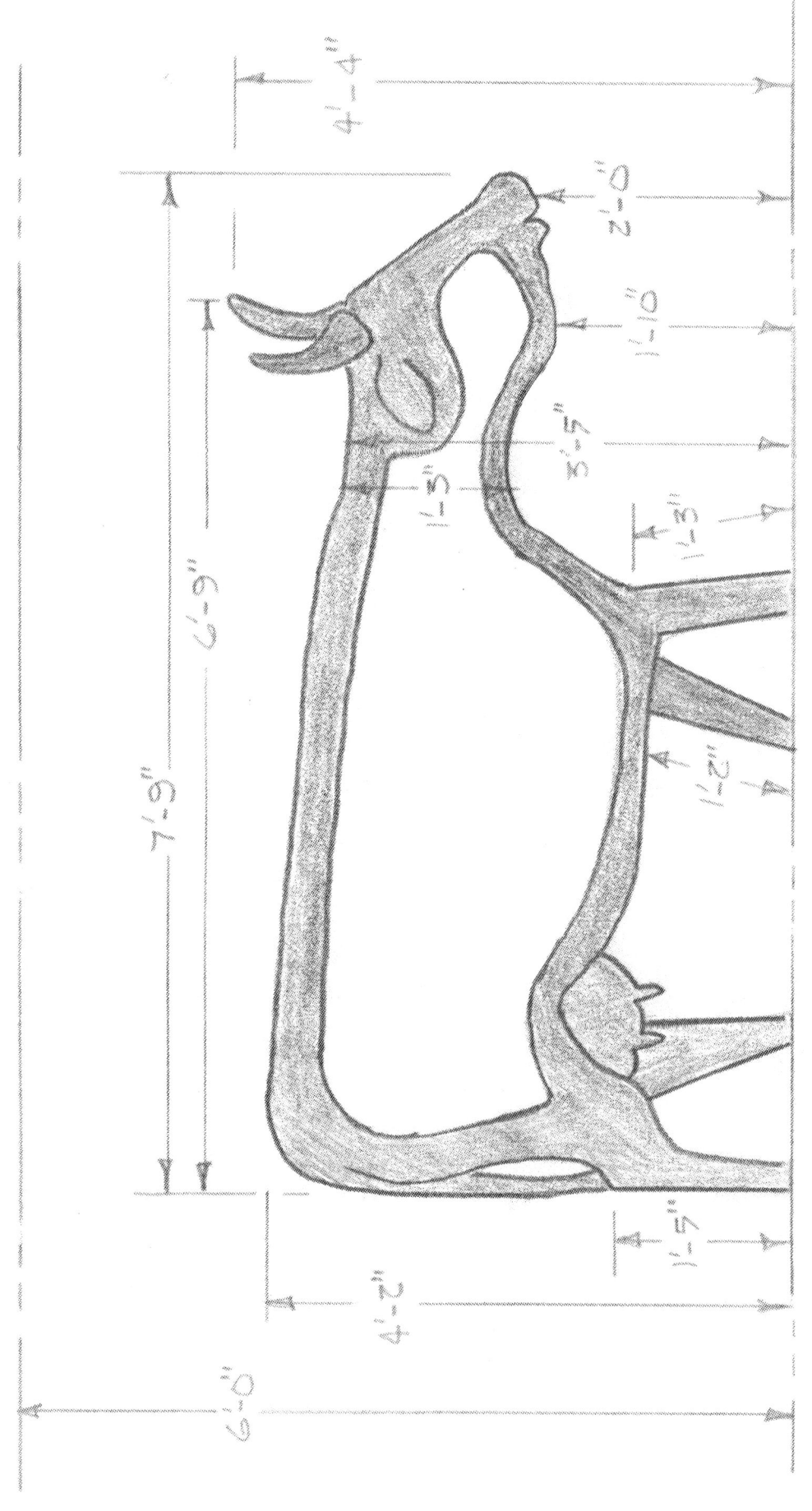

Cow In Stable — D

Donkey In Stable — E

3'-6"

1'-3"

1'-9"

5'-0"

8"

1'-1"

6'-9"

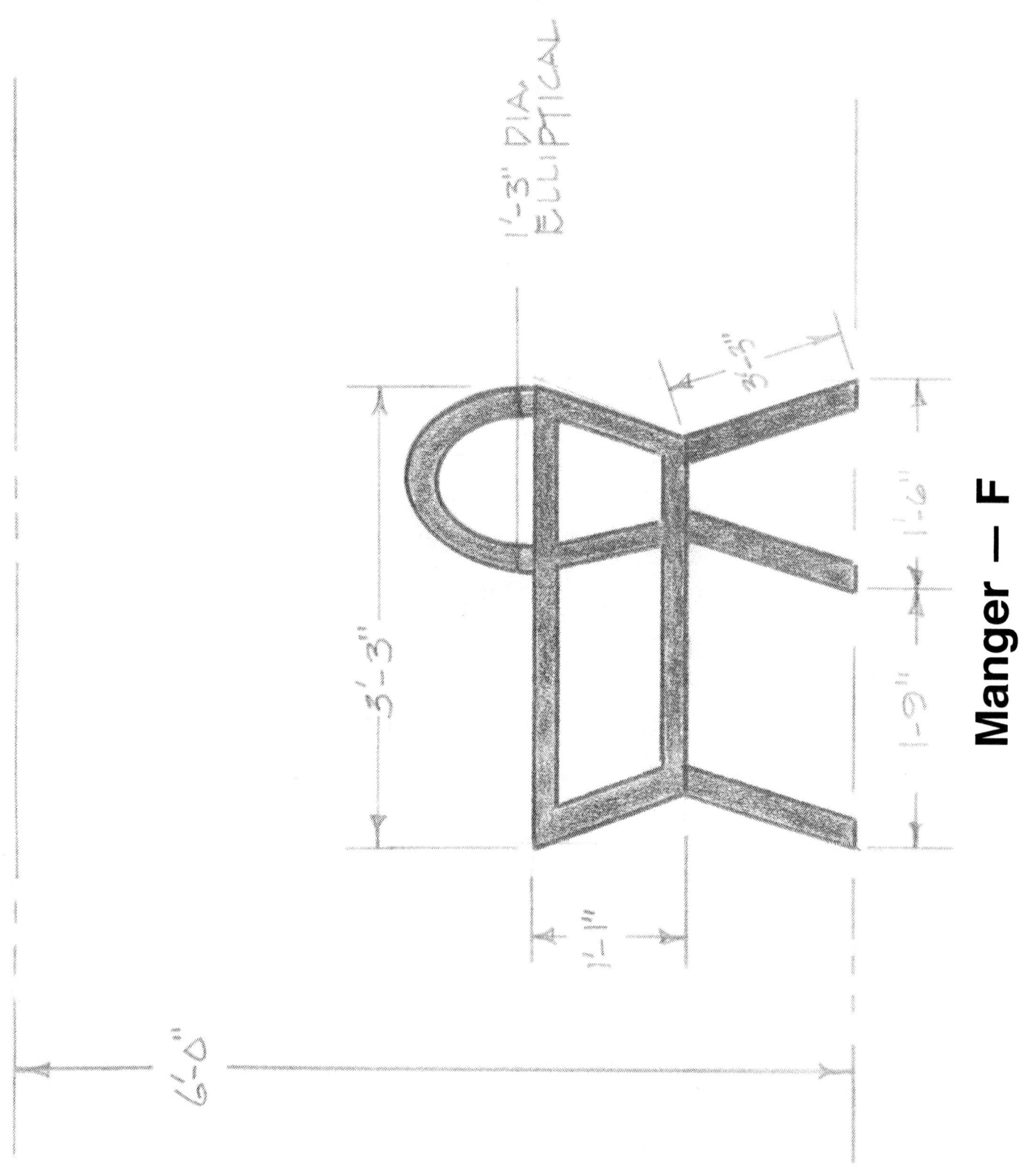

Manger — F

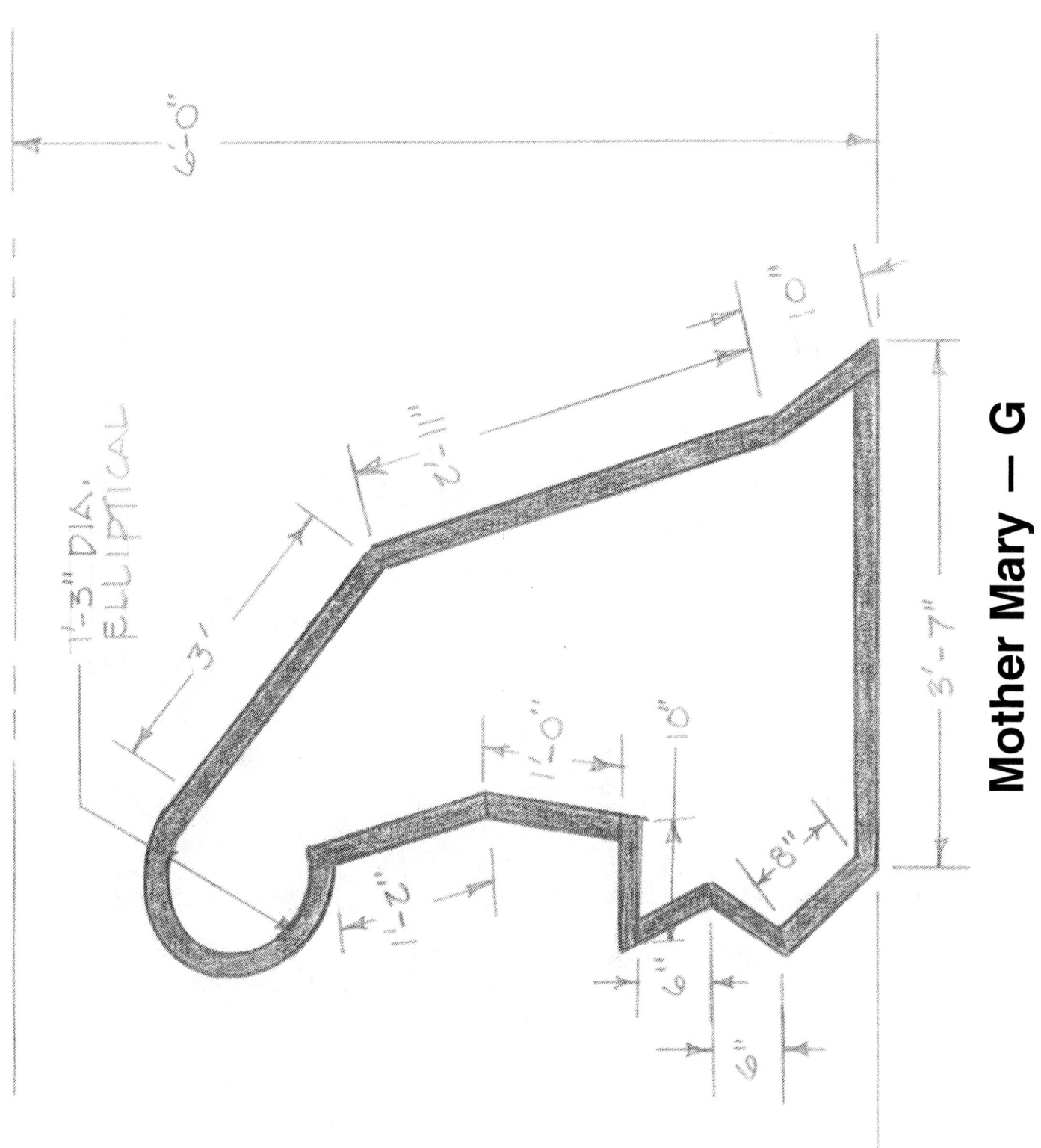

Mother Mary — G

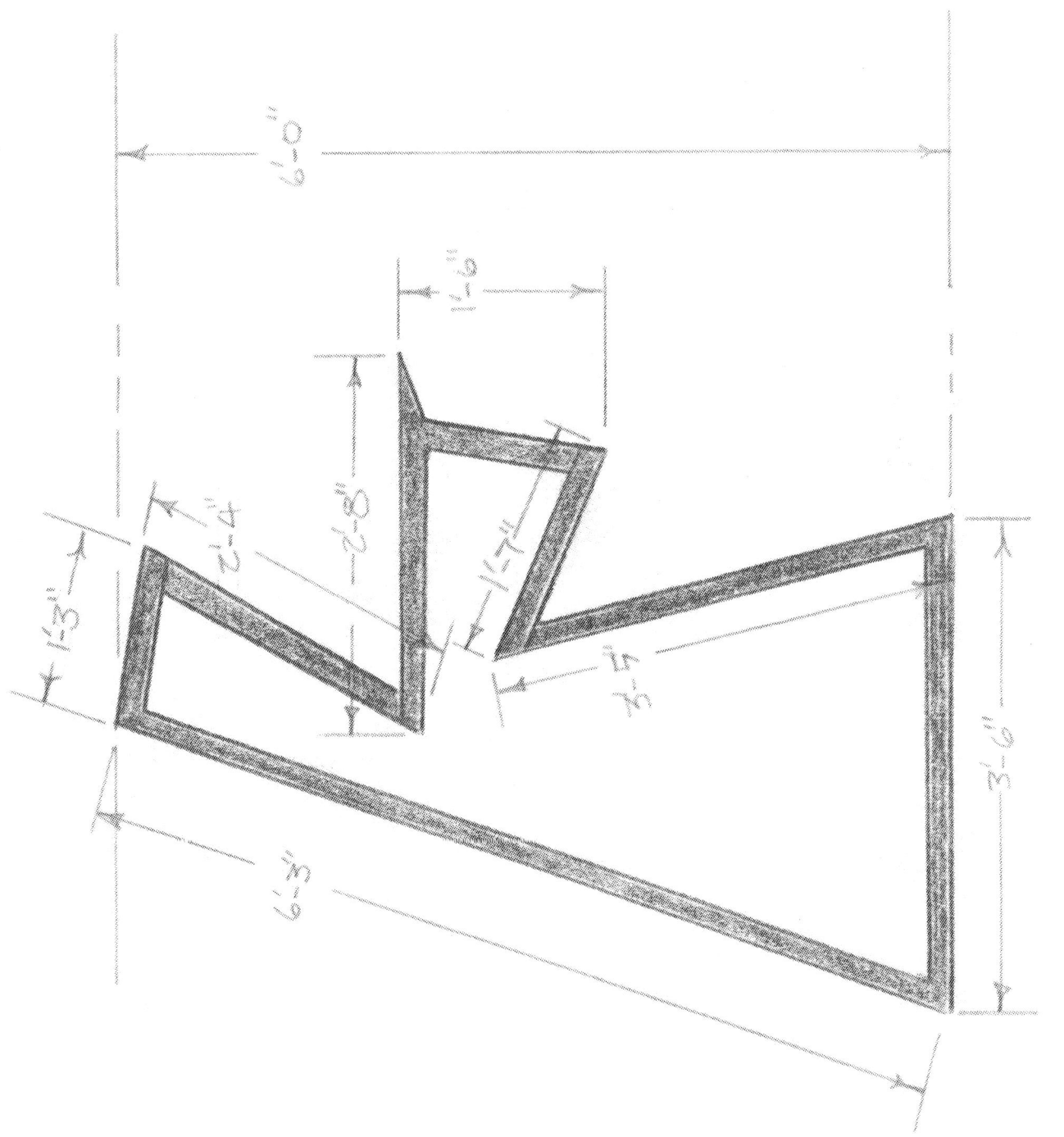

Joseph — H

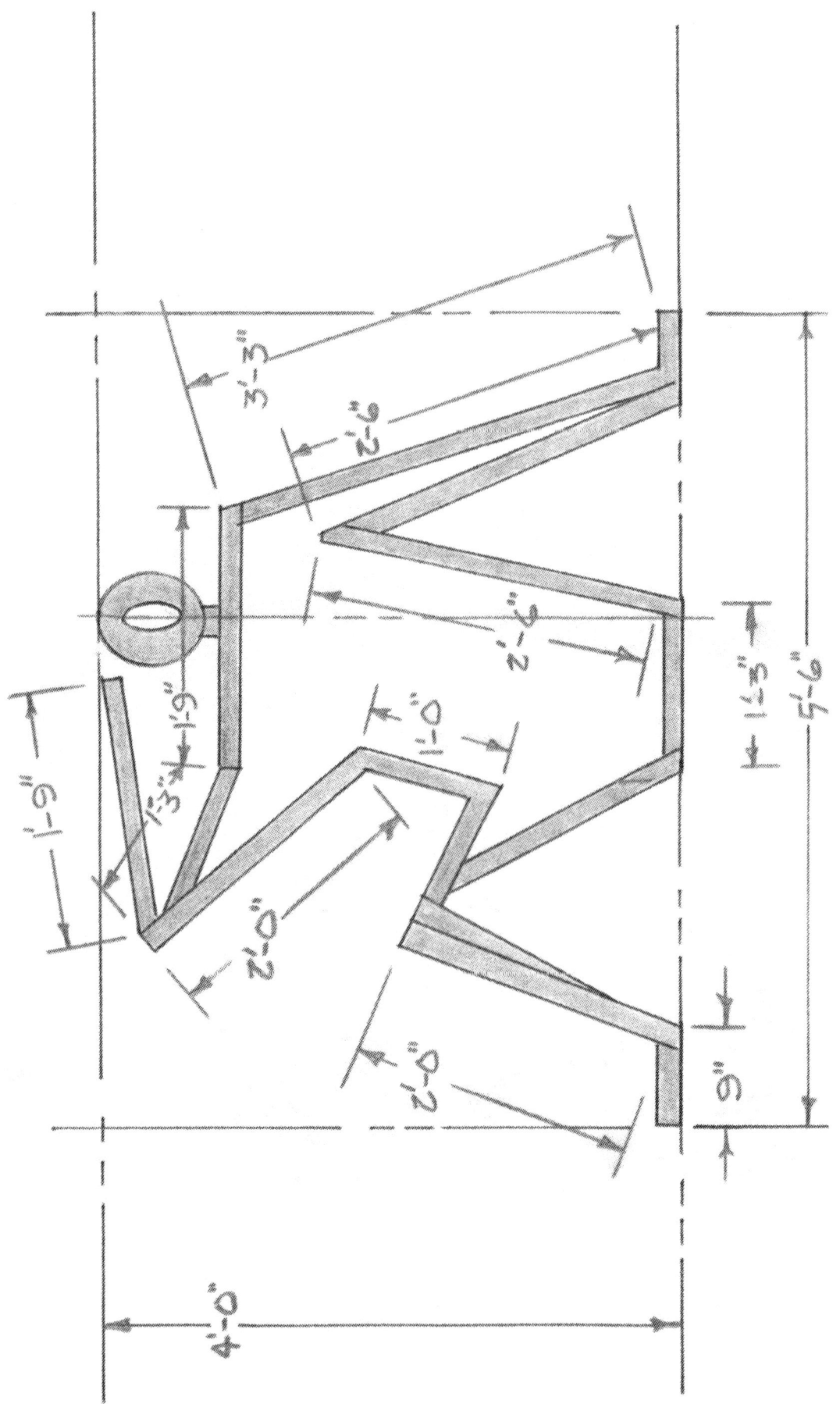

Amazed Shepherd – 1

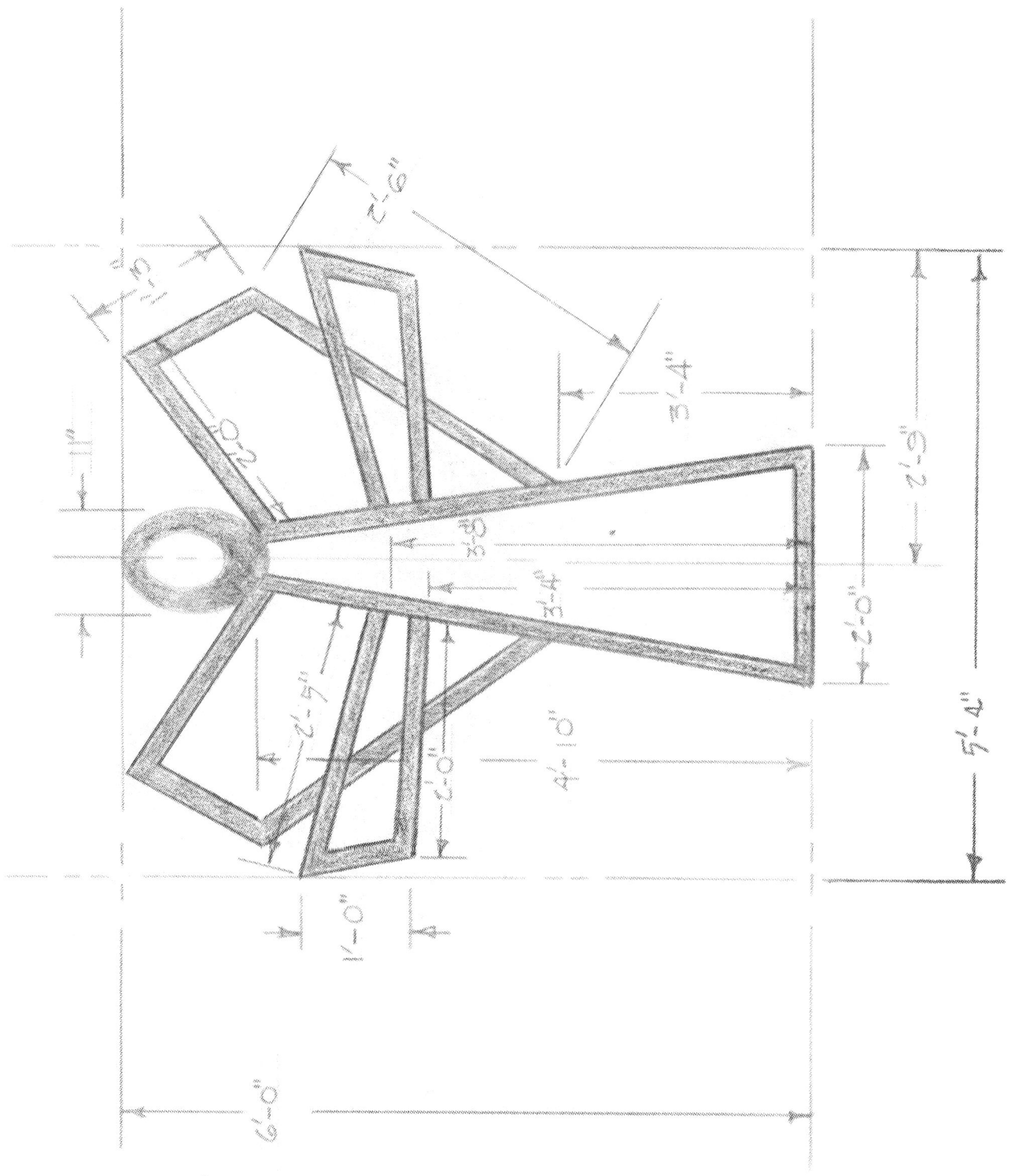

Angel — J

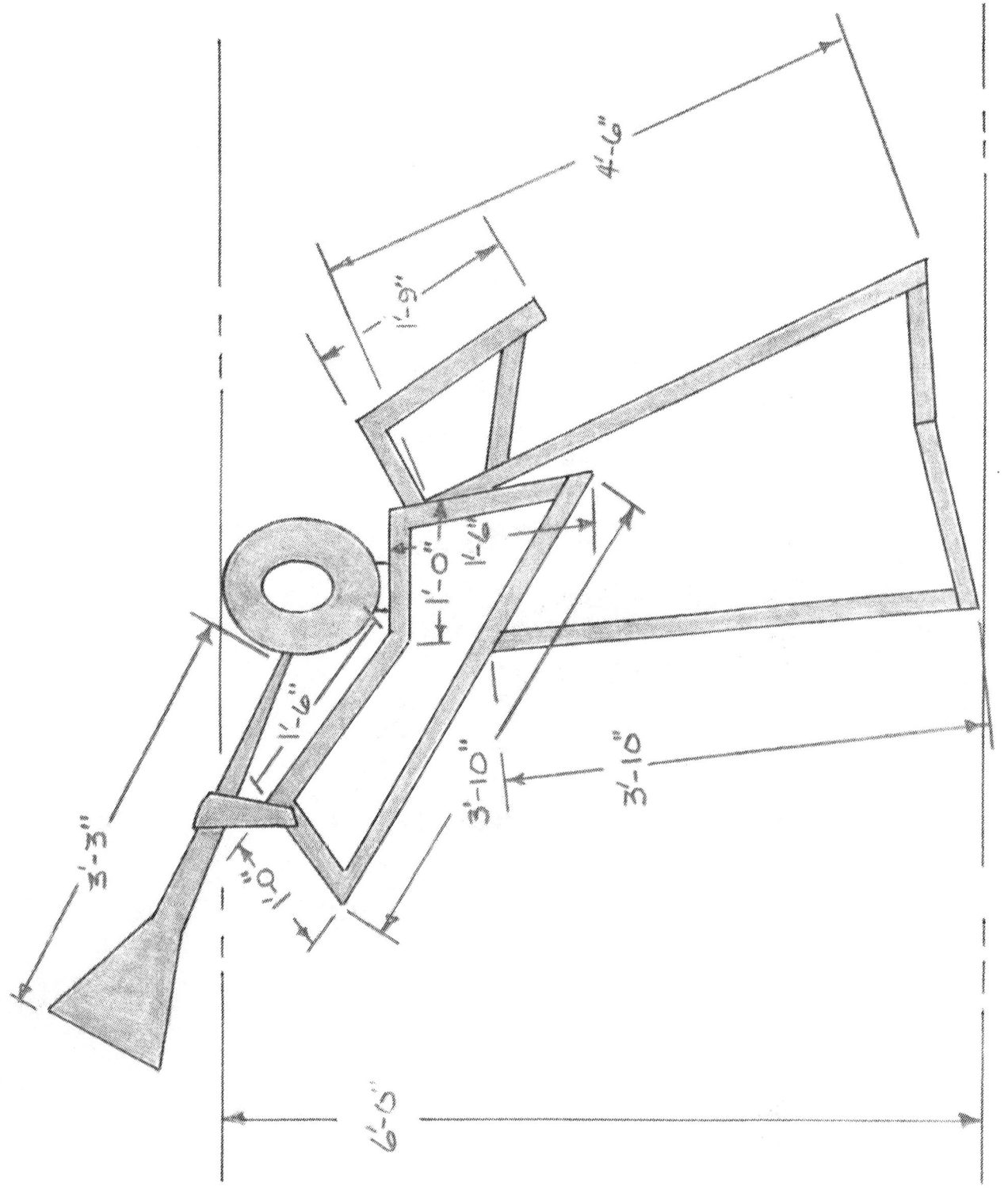

Angel With Trumpet – K

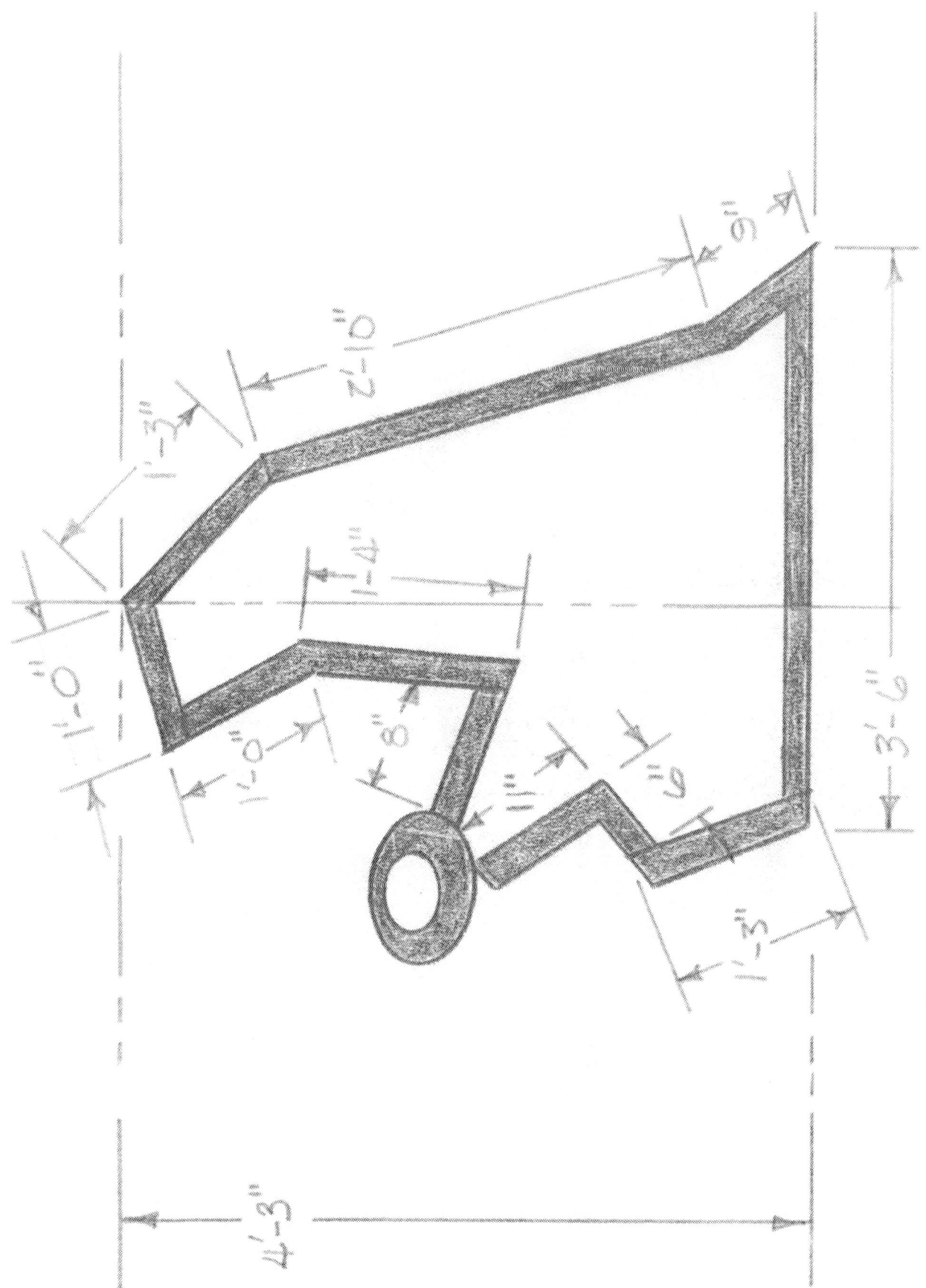

Adoring Mary And Jesus — L

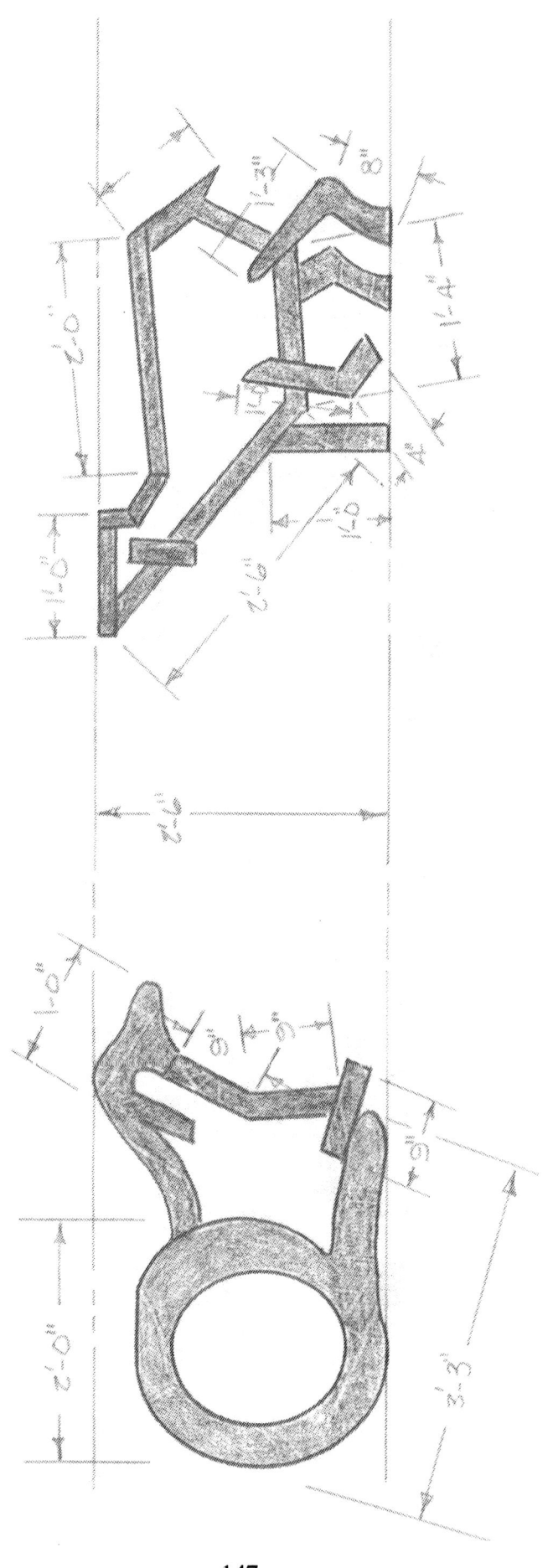

Two Sheep — M

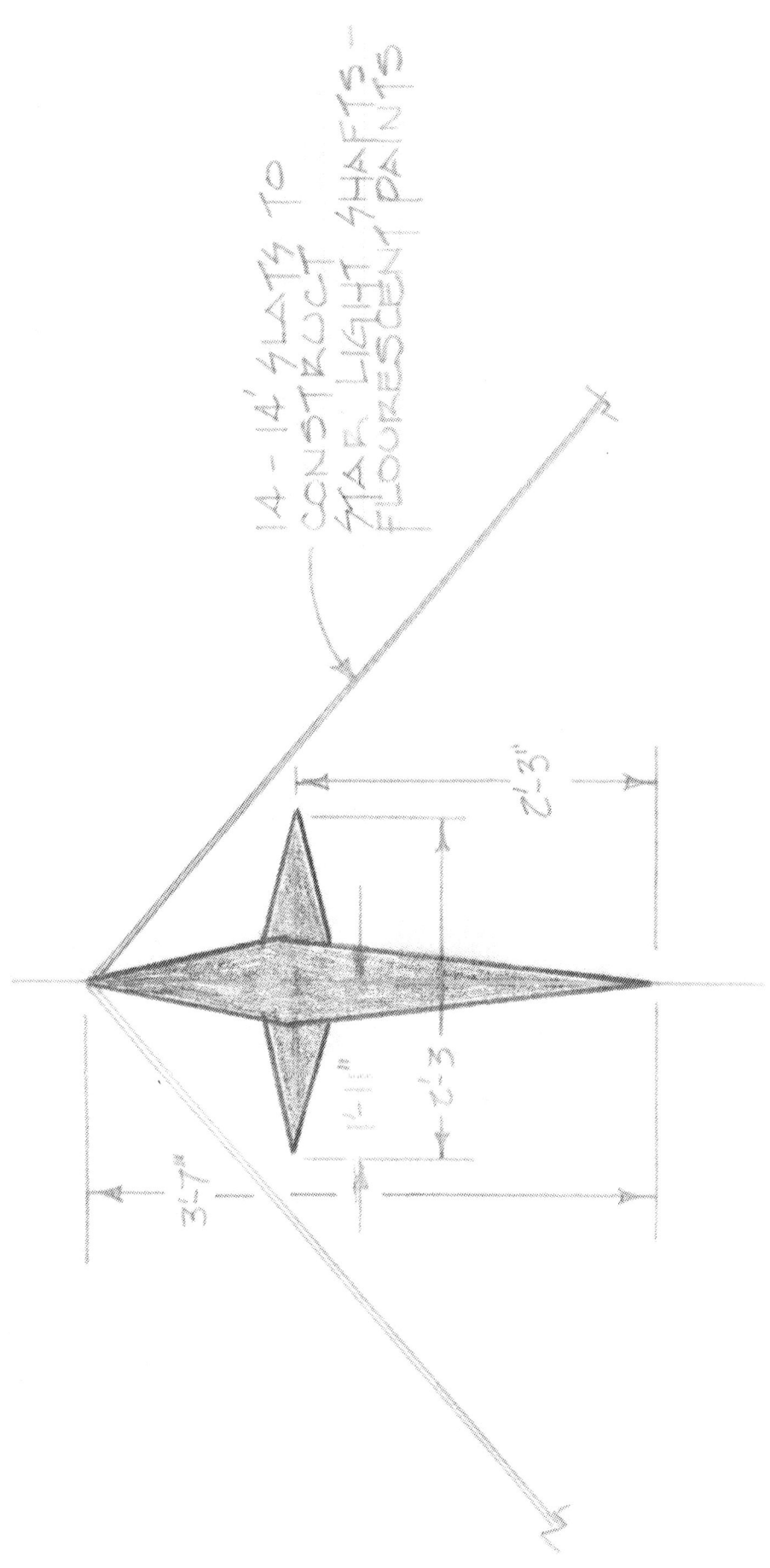

Star – N

Photo 1

Photo 2

Photo 3

A Christmas Program

Format

A Christmas Program

Narration: We begin our Christmas worship and pageant tonight with the wondrous images of Luke, chapter 2, dancing in our eyes and warming our hearts. We gather to worship. We gather to honor. We gather to celebrate the birthday of Jesus at Bethlehem, the Messiah, our Christ.

Christmas Puppet Play

Narration: Jesus Christ is the gift of gifts. How amazing when the prophets Isaiah, Micah, and others foretold of the coming of the one who would bring deliverance to the people of Israel. The immediate deliverance was for the Israelites to be freed from bondage in exile. The long-term deliverance applied to all people in bondage to sin, death, and the power of the devil.

A deliverer would come who would be born in Bethlehem and who would be the Savior, not only for the Jewish people, but for the whole world. The babe, Jesus, born in a stable and laid in an animal's manger would be, and is, God's gift to the world — and God's gracious and everlasting gift to you and me.

As you give your offering tonight, let your gift be a way of saying simply, "Thank you." Your gift will be used in the ministry of Christ through this congregation.

The birth of Jesus was not fable nor a made-up tale. The Nativity of our Lord Jesus was, and is, a real-life, flesh-and-blood story of the Incarnation of God in human affairs. Jesus would be declared Christ the King.

One of the characters in the birth-of-Jesus story had a strong opinion about a certain rumor that a new king of the Jews had been born. Let's listen in.

Herod's Monologue

Narration: I would have been afraid of King Herod, wouldn't you? He was insanely paranoid. He would not stand any rivals to his throne. He's resting now — asleep — perhaps harmless. Now he can't do much harm, but I'm sure he'll think of some treachery later.

Now, if you and I had traveled to Bethlehem in those days, we might have met this man. Careful — he sounds a bit put out. Maybe this traveling season with the census and all, has made him tired and crabby.

Innkeeper's Monologue

Joseph's Monologue

Narration: There were shepherds guarding their flocks out on those Judean hills. That is in itself nothing unusual. Shepherds have been doing that for hundreds of years. But shepherds were not considered very highly. They came from the lower class. They smelled, they were not always clean, and yet to those rather lowly, unpretentious folks, God visited that holy night. Amazing!

Shepherd's Monologue

Narration: That night was an amazing night. It was the greatest event in human history. God put on bands of cloth and God became one of us and they knew it. The angels knew it and they sang, "Gloria in excelsis" for the world to hear forever.

Angel's Monologue

Mary's Monologue

(After this monologue, Mary and Joseph may walk around and share the Baby Jesus with the audience.)

The End

Puppet Play

Christmas Puppet Play

Characters:
    Odie (dog)
    Carl (crocodile)
    Frieda (frog)
    Roger (dog) — nonspeaking
    Lizzie (disheveled puppet, dowdy, poor) — nonspeaking
    Paul (puppy) — nonspeaking

(The play opens with Odie and Carl talking.)

Odie: I can hardly wait. I'm so excited. It's almost here ... Christmas! Oh, my — oh, me. I can't stand it. I get to open *presents*!

Carl: Presents? Did someone say *presents*?

Odie: Yes, I did. Do you like presents, too, Carl?

Carl: Do I like presents? Is the pope Catholic? Are crocodiles green? I love presents almost more than anything. I hope to get tons of them for Christmas.

Odie: Me, too, Carl, me, too. I hope I get truckloads. I hope I get 497 presents this Christmas.

Carl: Yo, I wonder if we are the only boys who like presents for Christmas? Look out there at all the boys and girls. Do you think that they just love presents, too?

Odie: I don't know. Let's ask them. Hey, dudes and gals, do you just *looove* presents, too? Clap your hands, stomp your feet, and yell out, "Merry Christmas," if you like presents.

(Odie and Carl wait for audience response.)

Carl: Yep. They are nuts over presents, too. Hey, Odie, what do you hope you get for Christmas?

Odie: Well, Carl, that's easy. I have my list right here. Let's see ... five dozen dog biscuits ... 46 chewy bones ... a plastic fire hydrant ...

Carl: *(interrupts)* Okay, okay. Your list is extremely long. Here's what I want: my own personal river to swim in ... 500 chocolate-covered fish ... 17 large toothbrushes ... a large mud bath ... and, and ...

(Frieda enters, interrupting Carl.)

Frieda: Hi, guys! Whatcha doin'?

Odie: Hi, Frieda. Carl and I are comparing our Christmas lists. We want lots and lots of presents. Here, look at our lists.

Frieda: Oh, my goodness. Those are mighty *looooong* lists, if you ask me. There's a ton more than you need or can even use. Five hundred chocolate-covered fish, five dozen dog biscuits, and ... I can't believe it.

Carl: Yeah, we could get sick on all that. Do you think it's a bit outrageous?

Frieda: Yep.

Odie: Well, I'll just put the best presents in the living room and the rest I'll put away in the closet.

Carl: I'll just keep the best presents and put the rest under my bed.

Frieda: That's impossible. You know why? Because the *best* present at Christmas is a little baby that was born a long time ago.

Odie and Carl: What?

Frieda: That's right. The best present didn't make your list. The best present at Christmas is a little baby that was born a long time ago.

Odie and Carl: What? A baby? What baby? Did Santa and Mrs. Claus have a baby?

Frieda: No, silly. You know. The baby Jesus was born in a stable in Bethlehem. And he came to save us from our sins and to be our friend. Christmas is the birthday of Jesus, our Lord.

Carl: Oh, yeah. I almost forgot. Thanks for reminding us again, Frieda. We had just been to Toys R Us and could only think of our material presents. Yep, Jesus is the best gift at Christmas. How could we forget?

Odie: Yo, Carl. I just thought of something. Rather than putting some of our presents in the closet or under the bed, let's share some of them with people who never get any presents.

Carl: That's a great idea, Odie. You know, we could also give the needy some other gifts this Christmas, too ... like our friendship ... our love and stuff like that. Oh, look, there's Roger.

(Roger enters.)

Odie: Yeah, Roger looks lonely. You know he never seems to have any friends. He is a bit odd, maybe even weird. Never combs his hair. Ears are different colors, too. But, Roger is a nice dog ... just lonely.

Carl: You're right, Odie. Let's make friends with him this Christmas. Let's invite him to play with us and come over to our house. We could even share one or two of our presents with him.

Frieda: Aha, now you're getting it. Now you're starting to see what Christmas is really all about.

Odie: Oh, look, there's Lizzie.

(Lizzie enters.)

Carl: Lizzie sure looks sad. Always wears those out-of-date clothes. I understand her dad is out of work. They only eat peanut butter and jelly sandwiches for every meal.

Odie: That's sad. We have so much food at our house. Sure the prices are going up, but we never, ever, go hungry. We could share some, easily, and maybe my little sister could play with her and make her happy.

Carl: Great idea, Odie. You know, I think that is really what Christmas is about. Oh, look, there's Paul.

(Paul enters.)

Odie: He looks bummed. What happened to him?

Carl: I heard he's been sick. Why don't we take him for a ride this afternoon and see how he's feelin'?

Odie: Let's do that. You know, Carl, we've been very selfish. All those presents. I feel better about Christmas when I see people in need and decide to help them.

Carl: Me, too.

Frieda: Well, now these two are on the right track. Looks like the Holy Spirit has helped them to see what Christmas is all about. It's all about Jesus and sharing and love. Christmas is not as much about getting as it is about giving. Thank God for the best present of all — the gift of Jesus, our Savior. Happy birthday, Jesus, happy birthday.

The End

Adapted from a play by James Donald.

Monologue

Herod's Monologue

I trust my presence here requires no introduction! I am, after all, the king of Judea!

I've been hearing rumors about some so-called king to have been born in Bethlehem, of all places. I know I may be paranoid, and it's really foolish for me to give this matter any more thought.

It could be a trap. Yeah, that's it, a trap. They're trying to distract me with all this mumbo-jumbo so I won't be aware of real trouble elsewhere. Ya know, I'll bet it's my rascally sons, once again trying to prove I've lost my mind. They accuse me of having gone off the deep end. So I'm a little eccentric, I know. But after all, I am their king. I'm entitled to govern as I please. How dare they question my authority! I am *their king*! Why must I put up with these babbling idiots? Still, I can't allow these rumors of a new king to continue. I must organize my spies and put a stop to this uprising before things get out of hand. These rumors must be stopped.

If only I could trust someone. Why am I surrounded by such incompetence? Time — that's what I need — time. I'll figure something out and put a stop to all this talk of a new great and mighty king of the Jews by myself.

I'm tired. I'll worry about this tomorrow. I've worked too hard today. I must rest now. Tomorrow ...

Written by Mary Jo Hensel.

Monologue

Innkeeper's Monologue

So you think it's easy being an innkeeper? Huh! It's enough to drive a person crazy. I don't know why I put up with them. Nothing I do is ever right. They complain about the food, the service, and, of course, the accommodations. I'm referring to all these demanding pilgrims who are coming to Bethlehem to register. My life has been turned upside down for weeks now.

If that's not enough, now I've got the town mad at me, too. The way they act you'd think I was the only one in town who could have given that Nazarean couple a room. It was likely that mine wasn't the only door they knocked on.

I feel like I'm trying to justify my turning them away, but it's not like I was lying to that young couple. My place honestly was full, and with her being so pregnant, she wouldn't have gotten a moment's rest here with all the drinking and carousing the soldiers were doing. I felt so badly when I shut the door; they looked like such nice people. It was obvious they were exhausted from their travels.

Later that night, I went outside to do some chores and they were still there. I could see it was too late for her. No way they could have moved on. I was embarrassed to suggest it, but there was a stable out back and the animals would keep them warm. It wasn't much, but it was better than having that poor baby outside — that sweet, young thing. I scrounged up an old blanket for her, and found them some leftovers from the kitchen. They were so grateful — can you believe it?

I've thought about that young couple often since that night. I don't know what it was, but there was something very special about them. I sure hope things worked out for them.

Written by Mary Jo Hensel.

Monologue

Joseph's Monologue

Life has been hard. I had to move from my hometown of Bethlehem to Nazareth just to make a living. I'm a carpenter by trade.

I had asked Mary to be my wife and things seemed to be going quite well for us until she went to see her cousin, Elizabeth. Mary was gone for three months. When she returned, I did not know what to do. She was pregnant. If this had happened to you, what would you have done? I was so upset and angry. How could Mary do this to me? I had made plans to call the engagement off. I did not want any court proceedings that would be damaging to her. If I publicly denounced her, she would have been stoned to death by the old Levitical law. I was scared. I was unsure. And then would you believe it, a presence, like an angel, came to me in a dream, telling me not to be afraid and to go ahead and take Mary as my wife. Mary had conceived the Son of God through the power of the Holy Spirit. The angel even told me our son would be named Jesus, and would be the Messiah. All of this sounds strange, but you know, my fears were calmed that night. I believed this was the word of God.

Then, wouldn't you know it? Emperor Augustus sent out a decree that all the world should be taxed. That meant we must make the trip to Bethlehem. I could not leave Mary behind, since there was no one but me to look after her. So we set out on foot for the "house of bread"; that's what Bethlehem means. I looked forward to getting back to my hometown, but when we got there, we had no place to stay. The town was full. Every inn was occupied. I hoped someone would take pity on Mary and me, since she was really pregnant. We ended up here in this stable — no heat — no light — no running water. And right here Mary gave birth do Jesus. We wrapped him up tightly to keep him warm and laid him in the manger of the oxen.

It's all so overwhelming; this new life left in our care, to instruct and guide and protect until he reaches adulthood. Mary is right and I wasn't hallucinating — there is something holy, something divine, in this little child. I know God will find a way to guide Mary and me as we raise this little Jesus boy. It's been a long night. Come over here with me and take a look at this child.

Written by Julie Rogness.

Monologue

Shepherd's Monologue

I'm a shepherd. I've been a shepherd in these Galilean hills for most of my life. I've got nearly fifty ewes and three buck sheep. You can see my flock over yonder munching whatever green sprouts they can find. I bought some hay from an innkeeper in Bethlehem. He stores it for the animals he keeps in the stable near his inn.

Ah yes, I love the life of a shepherd. Gets crazy once in a while when I've got to chase away a wolf or a lion or a rustler. No wild beasts or thief is going to get away with any of my flock as long as I have this staff and this club. *(shows staff and club)*

Now, let me tell you what happened one night when my shepherd friends, Josh, Tobias, Shilock, and I were watching our flocks. We suddenly heard singing. We were confused at first. We wondered where in the blazes it was coming from. The singing was gorgeous — perfect harmony. And then there was a light — a bright light from above. The whole countryside must have heard the singing and seen the light. Then we heard a voice instructing whoever could hear it to go into town and see a newborn baby and his mother and father. We sensed that we were to go to the innkeeper's stable, the same one where we had purchased our hay, and so, shaking in our sandals, we went. What we saw was both usual and unusual.

After we left, we realized that shepherding sheep would never be quite the same. We had seen, there in the stable, in a manger in the same hay our sheep relished, a newborn child who would one day change the world.

Monologue

Angel's Monologue

The Lord of the universe announced to our choir that singing was needed for a most special event. So all of us angels, many thousands, both seraphim and cherubim volunteered. It was to be the greatest event in human history. We were to sing the "Gloria In Excelsis." We had practiced it for more than eight millennia and we were ready. Gabriel and Asaph and the harp section were ready, too. So down to earth we went. We would speak and *sing* our message.

My name is Angela. My name comes from what I am — an angel. *Angelos* means "messenger," and my whole existence has been dedicated to carrying messages from the Lord to humans on earth.

I was thrilled. That was the greatest night we angels have ever experienced. We were awestruck that our Lord would step down and become a little child.

We understand that the response has been mixed. Many people have begun to believe and to follow our Lord Jesus, while others — well, let's say, they're puzzled about it all.

Monologue

Mary's Monologue

It all seems so unbelievable now. How could all of this have happened to me? I am the daughter of a common man in a small village. My parents died when I was young and I was considered the lowliest one of all, a mere servant. I live in the village of Nazareth. I tended cattle and the house as well as doing other chores. I was a teenager when this all began. The angel Gabriel, so they called him, came to tell me I had favor with God and would become pregnant and bear God's Son. I was stunned. I kept saying over and over, "But how can this be?"

I left town to spend some time with my cousin, Elizabeth. Elizabeth is a favorite older relative who was unable to bear children. But can you imagine, much to my surprise, when I arrived at her home, she proudly announced that she was six months' pregnant. During my three months with Elizabeth, talking sometimes deep into the night, I knew that with God, nothing is impossible. God, my Savior, had remembered me, his lowly servant girl.

I was so nervous about returning to Nazareth pregnant, unmarried, and engaged to Joseph. What would my beloved Joseph think? What would he do? Would he still want to marry me, a virgin, who was pregnant with God's Son?

Joseph has been very understanding and caring through this whole ordeal. He even brought me along to Bethlehem so he could care for me as my time was nearing. I'm only a teenager and I must admit it was scary to give birth to my first son and, of all places, in a stable. I needed help in knowing how to take care of this new baby. He's so tiny, so precious, and so dependent on me.

I'm so exhausted now from the travel and now the birth. I feel both excitement and fear. I want to celebrate and sleep at the same time. Oh, my Lord, I hope I can do this. I sure wish that Elizabeth or someone could have been here to help.

The prophet Isaiah's words were surely fulfilled: "Unto us a child is born, unto us a Son is given." I hope and pray you will always remember and believe that this Son of God is yours, too — for unto you a Son is given.

Written by Julie Rogness.

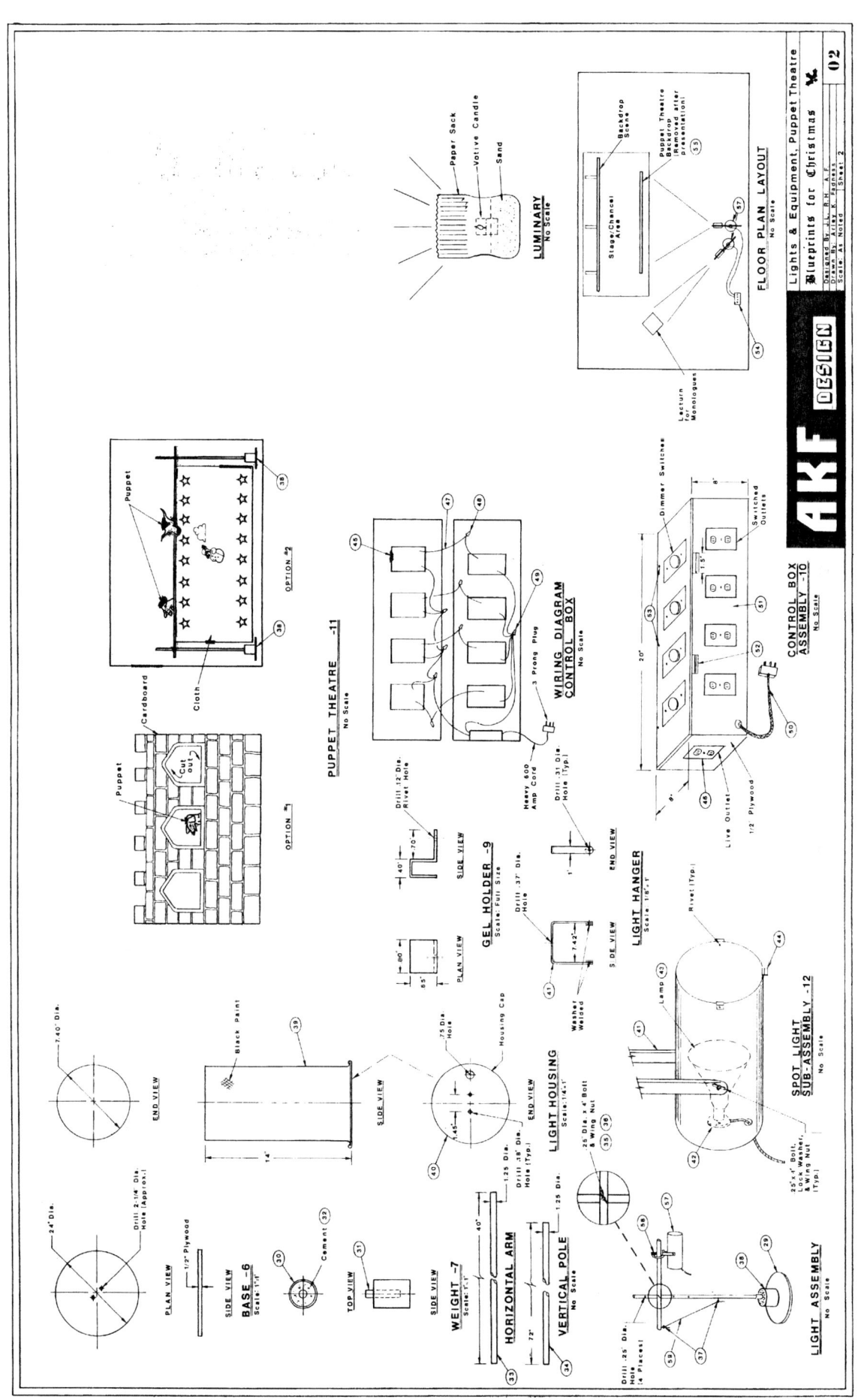

Materials List

Item	Description	Quantity	Blueprint No.
1	muslin cloth	as required	01
2	light neutral flat latex paint	as required	01
3	medium brown paint	as required	01
4	light brown paint	as required	01
5	black paint (for accent)	as required	01
6	beige paint	as required	01
7	light blue paint	as required	01
8	light green paint	as required	01
9	1/2" plywood gusset -1	12	01
10	1/2" plywood joiner strip -2	18	01
11	1/2" x 6" strap hinge - right	10	01
12	1/2" x 6" strap hinge - left	10	01
13	backdrop panel sub-assembly -3	3	01
14	back brace sub-assembly -4	3	01
15	1" x 10" x 13" wood base	3	01
16	1" x 10" x 5' - 4" wood base	3	01
17	1/4" x 1" eye bolt	3	01
18	2" x 2" angle iron	3	01
19	#7 nails or equivalent	as required	01
20	#8 wood screws or equivalent	as required	01
21	3/8" x 18" pipe	3	01
22	3/8" x 18" rod	3	01
23	5/16" set screw	3	01
24	cross brace sub-assembly -5	3	01
25	3/8" staples	as required	01
26	wheat paste or equivalent	as required	01
27	1" x 4" x 10' pine board	6	01
28	1" x 4" x 6' pine board	15	01
29	1/2" x 24" diameter plywood base -6	1 per unit	02
30	8" diameter metal can weight -7	1 per unit	02
31	1 1/3" diameter x 6" pipe	1 per unit	02
32	cement	as required	02
33	1 1/4" x 40" wood dowel	as required	02
34	1 1/4 " x 6' wood dowel	as required	02
35	1 1/4" x 4" screw	1	02
36	1/4" wing nut	1	02
37	eye screw	2	02
38	weight light standard sub-assembly -8	1 per unit	02
39	7.40" diameter x 14" cylindrical housing	1 per unit	02
40	7.50" ± diameter sheet metal circular	1 per unit	02
41	1/8" x 1" x 24.22" iron light hanger	1 per unit	02
42	lamp socket	1 per unit	02
43	spot lamp	1 per unit	02
44	gel holder -9	3 per unit	02
45	dimmer switch	4 per unit	02
46	duplex outlet	5 per unit	02
47	#14 wire	as required	02
48	electrical connectors	7	02
49	electrical cap	1	02
50	600 amp cord and 3-prong plug	1	02
51	1/2" x 8" x 20" plywood board	4 per unit	02
52	1 1/2" hinge	2 per unit	02
53	wood screws	as required	02
54	control box sub-assembly -10	1	02
55	puppet theater (options) -11		02
56	3/8" x 4" rod	3	01
57	spotlight sub-assembly -12	2	02
58	"C" clamp	2	02
59	wire or strong tie	as required	02
	luminary (optional)	as required	02

Construction Notes #02
Light Assembly
1. Construct spotlight(s) by building a base (-6), weight (-7), and poles as shown.
2. Paint black.

Spotlight Sub-assembly
1. Construct spotlight as shown (-12).
2. Install a 150 watt lamp.
3. Paint black.

Control Box Assembly
1. Construct control box as shown (-10).
2. Paint black.

Puppet Theatre
1. Two models shown (-11). Construct as appropriate.

Luminaries (Optional)
1. Luminaries may be used along the sidewalk or entrance to dramatize the pageant.
2. Luminaries are made of paper sacks, sand, and votive candles.